'The New ⌐ʝ⎯

'The New Syria?'

Critical perspectives on the deradicalisation
and reintegration of Islamist offenders

Edited by Emma Webb

CIVITAS

First published September 2020

© Civitas 2020
55 Tufton Street
London SW1P 3QL

email: books@civitas.org.uk

All rights reserved

ISBN 978-1-912581-17-7

Independence: Civitas: Institute for the Study of Civil
Society is a registered educational charity (No. 1085494)
and a company limited by guarantee (No. 04023541).
Civitas is financed from a variety of private sources to
avoid over-reliance on any single or small group of donors.

All the Institute's publications seek to further its objective
of promoting the advancement of learning. The views
expressed are those of the authors, not of the Institute.

Typeset by Typetechnique

Printed in Great Britain
by 4edge Limited, Essex

Contents

Authors

Emma Webb is the director of the Forum on Integration, Democracy and Extremism (FIDE) at Civitas, and editor of *Islamophobia: An Anthology of Concerns* (2019). Emma was formerly a research fellow at the Centre on Radicalisation and Terrorism at the Henry Jackson Society (HJS), where her research focused on how Islamist extremist groups in the UK and Europe establish and exploit organisations and institutions, extremist social networks, Islamist fundraising methods, counter-extremism policy and Prevent. Emma has widely advised the public sector on these issues, has featured on national and international media, and has written for *The Times*, *Daily Telegraph*, *Independent*, the *Spectator*, among others. She has an MA in Theological and Religious Studies from Trinity College Cambridge, and an MA from King's College London (KCL).

Jesse Morton was once a prominent jihadist radicalizer and recruiter in the West. As a co-founder and chief propagandist of Revolution Muslim, a New York City-based group active in the 2000s, he helped to insert the narrative of Al-Qaeda and Salafi-jihadist ideology into the American ambit. He is widely read in classical Islamic theology and jurisprudence, and historical relations between the United States and Middle Eastern nations. He is now a special advisor to CEP and is Executive Officer at Parallel Networks, a nonprofit dedicated to combating polarization, hate and extremism in the United States. Jesse holds a bachelor's degree in Human Services and a master's in International Relations from Columbia University, with a concentration on the Middle East and nonprofit management.

Ian Acheson is an Ulsterman with a long involvement in prison security and counter-terrorism. In 1994, he joined Her Majesty's Prison Service as a prison officer, rising rapidly to governor rank. On leaving the prison service, Ian was appointed director of the international prison charity Prisoners Abroad, supporting British citizens detained overseas. A spell as head of region for the government's Youth Justice Board in Southwest England led to a senior Civil Service role with the Home Office. In 2015, Ian led an independent review of Islamist extremism in prisons and probation in the UK. Ian has advised governments on countering violent extremism. He currently works as a senior adviser to the US-based Counter Extremism Project. He is visiting Professor at Staffordshire University school of Law, Policing and Forensics.

Dr Julia Rushchenko is an Associate Professor at the University of West London where she teaches Counter Terrorism and Organised Crime. She holds a PhD in Criminology from Utrecht University and previously has held a number of academic appointments in the Netherlands, Germany and the USA. Besides her academic expertise she regularly advises think tanks and NGOs on the issues of criminal justice, counter extremism and deradicalisation.

Liam Duffy is an advisor and researcher on extremism and counter-terrorism. He is also an adviser for the Counter Extremism Project, a New York based non-profit organisation and a Fellow of the Salzburg Global Seminar.

James Treadwell is Professor of Criminology in the School of Law, Policing and Forensics at Staffordshire University. He has also worked at the University of Birmingham, and University of Leicester. Previously he worked for the crime reduction charity NACRO and for the National Offender Management Service. His research largely centres around issues of Violent, Professional Crime and Organised Crime, Extremism Prison and Imprisonment (including Prison Violence and Victimisation). He has published several books on a range of crime subjects and numerous articles in leading international academic Journals such as the *British Journal of Criminology, Criminology and Criminal Justice, Deviant Behavor, Crime, Media, Culture* and the *Howard Journal of Criminal Justice.*

Acknowledgements

The editor would like to thank Jack Harris, research assistant to the Forum on Integration, Democracy and Extremism (FIDE).

Introduction: The need for critical perspectives on the deradicalisation and reintegration of extremist offenders

Emma Webb

Alongside returning foreign terrorist fighters (FTFs) and home-grown radicals, the threat posed by 'prison leavers' has long been on the radar, in both the United Kingdom and the rest of Europe.[1] As mounting challenges from extremism within the prison system – both behind bars and once released – demand solutions, we are in need of critical approaches that examine the underlying assumptions of accepted perspectives to assess what interventions are effective and why, what might be a waste of resources, and importantly, allowing for healthy scepticism about the limitations of 'deradicalisation' and what we mean when we use that term.

At the top of the agenda is the issue of false compliance – extremist offenders fooling rehabilitation programmes – which is widespread among jihadist prisoners, as reported by *The Times* in July 2020.[2] It is likely this news did not

---

[1] 'EU counter-terrorism chief: Europe 'may see something like Daesh 2.0', *Euractiv*, 12 December 2018, available at: https://www.euractiv.com/section/defence-and-security/interview/eu-counter-terrorism-chief-%D0%95urope-may-see-something-like-daesh-2-0/

[2] 'Terrorists fool prison staff into believing they have changed', *The Times*, 24 July 2020, available at: https://www.thetimes.co.uk/article/terrorists-fool-prison-staff-into-believing-they-have-changed-rb6tt0s66

come as a shock, to either professionals working in counter extremism or to the general public. The source of the story was a report published by the International Centre of the Study of Radicalisation and Political Violence (ICSR) at King's College London,[3] which found this to be a major issue in relation to risk assessment and release arrangements.[4]

This was particularly prescient in the UK context after the stabbing attack carried out by Usman Khan in November 2019 on London Bridge. Khan had been linked with the proscribed group Al Muhajiroun,[5] and was reportedly a student and close friend of the group's co-founder and leader, Anjem Choudary,[6] who was convicted in July 2016 for inviting support of Islamic State.[7] Khan had been jailed on terrorism-related charges in 2012.[8] However, released on licence halfway through his sentence, he carried out his successful 2019 attack less than a year after his release.[9]

Khan had participated in and completed the Healthy Identity Intervention Programme while in prison, and the Disengagement and Desistence programme after his release. Yet, when Khan attacked, killing two Cambridge University

---

[3] Rajan Basra and Peter R. Neumann, 'Prisons and Terrorism: Extremist Offender Management in 10 European Countries', *International Centre for the Study of Radicalisation* (2020), available at: https://icsr.info/wp-content/uploads/2020/07/ICSR-Report-Prisons-and-Terrorism-Extremist-Offender-Management-in-10-European-Countries_V2.pdf

[4] *Ibid.*

[5] 'London Bridge: Who was the attacker?', *BBC News*, 5 December 2019, available at: https://www.bbc.co.uk/news/uk-50611788

[6] 'Usman Khan: knifeman was friend of hate preacher Anjem Choudary', *The Times*, 30 November 2019, available at: https://www.thetimes.co.uk/article/usman-khan-who-was-the-knifeman-xsb8g72n2

[7] 'Profile: Anjem Choudary', Counter Extremism Project, available at: https://www.counterextremism.com/extremists/anjem-choudary

[8] 'Nine jailed over bomb plot and terror camp plan', BBC News, 9 February 2012, available at: https://www.bbc.co.uk/news/uk-16968518

[9] 'London Bridge attack: sentencing row – who did what?' *BBC News*, 1 December 2019, available at: https://www.bbc.co.uk/news/uk-50623821

students, Jack Merritt and Saskia Jones,[10] he did so while attending a conference at Fishmonger's Hall, London Bridge, that was organised by Cambridge University's 'Learning Together' scheme, intended to bring offenders together for study to 'break down prejudices and [create] new possibilities for all who took part'.[11]

It isn't hard to see how this tragic irony could have a powerful impact on the public experience of insecurity; while attending a conference celebrating success in deradicalizing people *like him*, an Islamist offender had thanked those who saw the best in him by murdering them in cold blood.

It left a lasting impression on practitioners and the public, leaving many wondering about the efficacy of deradicalisation programmes and the potential for extremist offenders to 'take us for a ride'. At the time, psychologist Christopher Dean, the designer of the Healthy Identity Intervention (HII) course – attended by Khan – was reported as having suggested that programmes cannot 'cure' extremist offenders.[12] The purpose of his course was, as the name suggests, intended to reduce recidivism among violent extremist offenders by re-examining their 'identity commitments'.[13] The medicalisation of language, at once reductive and abstract, is noticeable – could it be warping our understanding of the problem and making it more difficult for us to manage the threat?

Only months later, on 2 February 2020, Sudesh Amman

---

[10] 'London Bridge: What we know about the attack', *BBC News*, 3 December 2019, available at: https://www.bbc.co.uk/news/uk-50594810

[11] 'London Bridge attack: What is the Learning Together scheme?', *BBC News*, 1 December 2019, available at: https://www.bbc.co.uk/news/uk-50623646

[12] 'London Bridge attack: Terrorists may not be 'cured' by prison deradicalization schemes, senior pschyologist admits', *Independent*, 2 January 2020, available at: https://www.independent.co.uk/news/uk/home-news/london-bridge-attack-terror-deradicalisation-prison-a9267436.html

[13] *Ibid.*

launched a similar stabbing attack in Streatham, London. Like Khan, Amman had also recently been released from prison;[14] he had previously been arrested in May 2018 on suspicion of planning a terrorist attack, but was not charged on that account; instead he was prosecuted for possession and dissemination of terrorist material.[15] Amidst a heated public debate on how the country should deal with foreign fighters, with many extremist offenders due for release, it was clear that another threat loomed large.

Following the Streatham attack, former Met Police Assistant Commissioner Sir Mark Rowley, implied that in terms of future jihadist threat, prisons were the new Syria:

'I remember being asked by MPs a few years ago when I was in post about the threat of returning Jihadis from Syria, which is a concern, but I remember saying to them at the time that there will be more dangerous people coming onto the streets of the UK from UK prisons with terrorist conviction than have been returning from Syria. And sadly that seems to be what is happening at the moment'.[16]

How serious is the threat posed by these prisoners? A recent quantitative study by Robin Simcox and Hannah Stuart for *CTC Sentinel* examining twelve alleged terror plots or attacks in Europe involving jihadi prisoners or those who had been released, found that those who were prevented from travelling to fight abroad and those who returned

---

[14] 'Streatham terror attack: What we know about Sudesh Amman', *Sky News*, 7 February 2020, available at: https://news.sky.com/story/streatham-terror-attack-what-we-know-about-sudesh-amman-11925200

[15] 'Sudesh Amman: Who was the Streatham attacker?', *BBC News*, 3 February 2020, available at: https://www.bbc.co.uk/news/uk-51351885

[16] 'Streatham terror attack: Government to introduce emergency legislation to remove automatic early release for terrorists, *Daily Telegraph*, 3 February 2020, available at: https://www.telegraph.co.uk/news/2020/02/03/streatham-attack-stabbing-terrorist-london-incident/

from doing so where commonly involved in the attacks, most specifically, targeting police and prison guards.[17] Calculations based on a second data set by the authors supported findings elsewhere that,

> 'terrorist recidivism among UK offenders who are convicted of multiple terrorism offenses on separate occasions is low. However, if individuals who had a prior criminal record for criminal behavior interpreted as extremism-related but not terrorism-related are included, the rate of recidivism posed by jihadi prisoners/prison leavers – and subsequent scale of the threat – is appreciably higher.'[18]

The seriousness of the combined threat asks that we are willing to set aside certain presumptions in service of an honest, critical and even sceptical approach if we are to effectively reduce risk and assess how successful we might expect to be. Almost all European countries have rehabilitation programmes for extremist offenders that include: risk assessment and tailored interventions, including mentoring, structured dialogue tools and therapy.[19] Given the severity of the threat posed, it is vital that programmes to deradicalise and rehabilitate offenders are efficacious in reducing recidivism and that we have an grounded debate about the limits of effectiveness and how it can be measured, so that resources are not wasted on bogus schemes.

---

[17] Robin Simcox and Hannah Stuart, 'The thread from Europe's Jihadi Prisoners and Prison Leavers', *CTC Sentinel*, July 2020, volume 13, issue 7, available at: https://ctc.usma.edu/the-threat-from-europes-jihadi-prisoners-and-prison-leavers/

[18] Robin Simcox and Hannah Stuart, 'The thread from Europe's Jihadi Prisoners and Prison Leavers', *CTC Sentinel*, July 2020, volume 13, issue 7, available at: https://ctc.usma.edu/the-threat-from-europes-jihadi-prisoners-and-prison-leavers/

[19] Basra and Neumann, 'Prisons and Terrorism', ICSR (2020), available at: https://icsr.info/wp-content/uploads/2020/07/ICSR-Report-Prisons-and-Terrorism-Extremist-Offender-Management-in-10-European-Countries_V2.pdf

A holistic approach is also needed, that accounts for the likelihood of success or false compliance when prisoners are potentially ensconced within a social environment stacked against them having a change of heart or mind. In 2016, the Acheson review found that Muslim gang culture within prisons constituted part of the threat, including 'charismatic' Islamist extremist prisoners 'acting as self-styled "emirs" and exerting a controlling and radicalising influence on the wider Muslim prison population' and 'aggressive encouragement of conversions to Islam'.[20]

According to the review, there were attempts from Islamist prisoners to segregate by landing, wing or even prison; to prevent staff from searching them by claiming dress is religious, as well as problems relating to the intimidation of prison imams, exploitation of staff who fear being called racist, the availability of extremist literature and unsupervised worship, in which staff members were sometimes pressured to leave the prayer room.[21]

This situation clearly persists, as demonstrated by reports in early 2020 of activity at HMP Woodhill. In January that year, another al-Muhajiroun linked offender, Brusthom Ziamani, allegedly attacked prison officers at HMP Whitemore, after being jailed in 2015 for planning an attack on a British soldier.[22] Reports of Ziamani and his fellow inmate's activities at

---

[20] Ian Acheson, 'Summary of the main findings of the review of Islamist extremism in prisons, probation and youth justice', *Ministry of Justice*, August 2016, available at: https://assets.publishing.service.gov.uk/government/uploads/system/uploads/attachment_data/file/547032/acheson-review-summary-aug-2016.pdf

[21] Ian Acheson, 'Summary of the main findings of the review of Islamist extremism in prisons, probation and youth justice', *Ministry of Justice*, August 2016, available at: https://assets.publishing.service.gov.uk/government/uploads/system/uploads/attachment_data/file/547032/acheson-review-summary-aug-2016.pdf

[22] 'Prisoner accused of stabbing guards in suspected terror attack 'held sharia courts in his jail cell', *Independent*, 11 January 2020, available at: https://www.independent.co.uk/news/uk/crime/prisoner-terror-attack-sharia-courts-hmp-whitemoor-brusthom-ziamani-a9279586.html

another prison, HMP Woodhill, are revealing.[23] According to a former inmate, Ziamani was notorious for trying to convert his fellow prisoners to radical Islam.[24]

According to a *Times* investigation, along with others, Ziamani instituted sharia courts to judge other prisoners, where inmates would be brought before the court for things such as 'disgracing the month of Ramadan' or drinking alcohol. Ziamani reportedly patrolled the block to ensure no one broke their fast during Ramadan and had appointed himself 'chief of the Sharia police'.[25]

According to a fellow inmate, one prisoner would read from the Quran and announce that the brothers would decide the punishment: 'A hundred lashes or a beating?' He recalled how, after Ziamani had called for a beating, the condemned men were punched and kicked: 'the smaller one couldn't open his eye, it was swollen completely shut, so we made him tell the screws [pejorative term for a prison officer] he had fallen down the stairs'.[26] One inmate allegedly lectured Ziamani and another prisoner on how 'the Queen was a false monarch and an enemy of Islam who should be fought to the death', and offered another inmate a box of literature including *Milestones* by Sayid Qutb, which is banned in UK prisons.[27]

A former prisoner told *The Times* that the prisoners were split into factions, aligned with Al Qaeda or Islamic State,

---

[23] 'Islamist extremists hold sharia trials and groom young Muslims in British prisons', *The Times*, 23 December 2019, available at: https://www.thetimes.co.uk/article/islamist-extremists-hold-sharia-trials-and-groom-young-muslims-in-british-prisons-2pq7ptjtp

[24] *Ibid.*

[25] 'Queen is enemy of Islam and must die, says jail 'emir'', *The Times*, 23 December 2019, available at: https://www.thetimes.co.uk/article/prison-extremism-queen-is-enemy-of-islam-and-must-die-says-jail-emir-7d3ll7v0k?ni-statuscode=acsaz-307

[26] *Ibid.*

[27] *Ibid.*

vying for control of the high security wing – and that Ziamani had defected from the Islamic State to Al Qaeda faction.[28] Evidently, under such circumstances, the necessities of daily survival and social pressure will hardly be conducive to 'deradicalisation'. This is one reason why the government, in response to a 75% increase in prisoners convicted of terrorism-related offences in the three years up to April 2018, has explored the potential of Separation Centres in England and Wales to contain extremist influence and power within the system.[29] Nevertheless, under these circumstances any programme dealing with prisoners could not succeed if it is shallow or surface level: if there are incentives in pretending to comply, the appearance of compliance should be viewed with a healthy dose of scepticism.

It is for these reasons, and among others, that this anthology brings together critical perspectives from a range of former Islamist extremists and international experts on deradicalisation and reintegration, so that it may serve as a companion for those interested in a balanced approach to the ideas and assumptions that underly policy in this contentious area.

Can jihadists be deradicalised? How can we rehabilitate terrorist offenders? How can evidence be brought into policy? Why do we use certain terms when referring to these offenders and does our use of language cloud our understanding? Why are we failing to recognise and respond

---

[28] 'Queen is enemy of Islam and must die, says jail 'emir'', *The Times*, 23 December 2019, available at: https://www.thetimes.co.uk/article/prison-extremism-queen-is-enemy-of-islam-and-must-die-says-jail-emir-7d3ll7v0k?ni-statuscode=acsaz-307

[29] Beverly Powis, Keely Wilkinson, Sinead Bloomfield and Kiran Randhawa-Horne, 'Separating Extremist Prisoners: A process study of separation centres in England and Wales from a staff perspective', *Ministry of Justice* (2019), available at: https://assets.publishing.service.gov.uk/government/uploads/system/uploads/attachment_data/file/818624/separating-extremist-prisoners.pdf

adequately to the intellectual component in the motivation of these offenders? What under-recognised assumptions and ideas may be holding us back from developing a better approach? What, in this context, counts as an effective intervention and can it be reproduced? How are Islamist ideas interacting with prevalent ideas in the academy, in particular, criminology? How might extremist offenders be exploiting weaknesses in the way we deal with them, and how can we stop it?

Can Jihadists be 'Deradicalised'?
Jesse Morton

Can jihadists be 'deradicalised?' It's a question many have been asking, especially since a spate of terrorist attacks perpetrated by convicted jihadists in the United Kingdom between November 2019 and February 2020 induced the UK government to introduce legislation to delay the release of terrorist prisoners.[1] The debate around 'deradicalisation' fell off in the midst of concerns for Covid-19, but as governments throughout the West prepare to face the release of hundreds of terrorism-related offenders in ensuing years, it will be imperative to return to the discussion and improve recidivism reduction efforts that might prevent re-radicalisation under expected conditions of reciprocal radicalisation and rampant uncertainty.[2]

---

[1] 'Hundreds of former jihadis are set to be freed from jail. London terror attack shows the risks', *CNN*, 1 December 2019, available at: https://edition.cnn.com/2019/12/01/uk/london-bridge-attack-analysis-gbr-intl/index.html; 'UK plans to delay early release of terror offenders', *Financial Times*, 3 February 2020, available at: https://www.ft.com/content/6e300ec0-467e-11ea-aee2-9ddbdc86190d

[2] 'Hundreds of former jihadis are set to be freed from jail. London terror attack shows the risks', CNN, 1 December 2019, available at: https://edition.cnn.com/2019/12/01/uk/london-bridge-attack-analysis-gbr-intl/index.html; 'The far right and reciprocal radicalisation', *Homeland Security News Wire*, 4 September 2018, available at: http://www.homelandsecuritynewswire.com/dr20180904-the-far-right-and-reciprocal-radicalization; Simona Trip, Carmen Hortensia Bora, Mihai Marian, Angelica Halmajan and Marius Ioan Drugas, 'Psychological Mechanisms Involved in Radicalisation and Extremism. A Rational Emotive Behavioural Conceptualization', *Frontiers in Psychology*, 6 March 2019, available at: https://www.ncbi.nlm.nih.gov/pmc/articles/PMC6414414/pdf/fpsyg-10-00437.pdf

Most recently, on 9 June 2020, the House of Commons met, in part, to discuss the merits of a Counter-Terrorism and Sentencing Bill that would enhance the sentence duration for convicted terrorists.[3] Justice Secretary Robert Buckland told MPs that the recent attacks 'clearly demonstrated the need for terror offenders to spend longer in prison.' However, Labour MP David Lammy countered that the UK attackers were 'neither deradicalized nor deterred by their time inside,' which 'may have made them worse.' Instead, Mr. Lammy questioned why the government had not announced a 'coherent deradicalization strategy' to go alongside the Counter-Terrorism and Sentencing Bill. 'There is little use in increasing sentences if we are to release them just a few years later still committed to their hateful ideology, still determined to wreak havoc,' he added.

The question of whether incarcerated extremists can be 'deradicalised' is one that manifests in my mind all too regularly. I myself am a former jihadist, an American convert that once ran an organisation that spewed Bin Laden's hateful views on New York City streets, and all over the world online.[4] For me, it is personal. Today, I consider myself deradicalised. However, the question has also become an external one. I now provide mentoring and deradicalisation-related support services for other extremists: jihadist, white supremacist, anti-government, Involuntary Celibate (Incels) and others, many of whom have been imprisoned.[5] If there

---

[3] 'Anger at attacks by released terrorists 'must not distort lessons', government warned over proposed laws', *Independent*, 9 June 2020, available at: https://www.independent.co.uk/news/uk/home-news/terror-law-uk-attacks-government-counter-terrorism-security-bill-a9557346.html

[4] 'Once a Qaeda Recruiter, Now a Voice Against Jihad', *The New York Times*, 29 August 2016, available at: https://www.nytimes.com/2016/08/30/us/al-qaeda-islamic-state-jihad-fbi.html

[5] 'Combating Violent Extremism and Terrorism', *C-Span*, 4 November 2019, available at: https://www.c-span.org/video/?466011-1/combating-violent-extremism-terrorism

is no such thing as deradicalisation, then these efforts are for nothing.

A headline in *The Telegraph* that ran around the time of the UK recidivists' violence stated, 'I was in al-Qaeda, then spied for MI6 – I know deradicalisation doesn't work.'[6] The article made doubts about deradicalisation glaring and mirrored much of public opinion. Based on an interview with Aimen Dean, former al-Qaeda higher-up turned counter-terrorism asset, the article stated that there 'is no such thing as a rehabilitated jihadist.' While I understand the sentiment, it lacks needed nuance and runs the risk of deepening the post-release stigmatisation that can facilitate terrorist recidivism. My personal experience offers one example that might inform the discussion.

Having worked first to deradicalise myself, and now other extremists, I must say that I share in the scepticism, but it is first imperative to add nuance by distinguishing between disengagement and deradicalisation.[7] Terrorism researchers identify disengagement as behavioural change, a breaking off of participation with an extremist organisation, while deradicalisation represents a deeper, cognitive alteration, a reorientation in belief or ideology. It is not an event; it is a process, a much longer process. Between disengagement and deradicalisation there are myriad steps and stages. To understand the processes associated with full-blown deradicalisation, however, we would do well to avoid analysing radicalised individuals as if they exist in isolation of culture and context.

---

6 "I was in al-Qaeda, then spied for MI6 – I know deradicalization doesn't work", *Daily Telegraph*, 8 February 2020, available at: https://www.telegraph.co.uk/men/thinking-man/al-qaeda-spied-mi6-know-deradicalisation-doesnt-work/

7 John Horgan, *Walking Away from Terrorism: Accounts of Disengagement from Radical and Extremist Movements* (Oxford, 2009)

Jihadist rehabilitation and reintegration is 'context-fluid,' a term designers use when a person uses a product (or a program) in a variety of scenarios and the outcomes, or experience with that product is heavily affected by the context.[8] The transnational appeal of jihadism ebbs and flows according to whether jihadists are perceived to be winning. However, all jihad is also local, and many terrorism-related convicts will be returning to communities that facilitated their initial radicalisation, and now to societies ravaged by internal discord and suffering from Covid-related socioeconomic frustration. Few reintegrating jihadists will be able to recognise that these same cultural and contextual influences can trigger an abandoning of realisations that often occur when one is incarcerated.

Usman Khan, who was convicted of plotting a terrorist attack in 2012 but recidivated and carried out a knife attack near London Bridge which killed two and wounded three on 29 November 2019, offers a pertinent example.[9] At the time of his criminal conviction, Khan wrote a letter from prison that stated, 'after spending some time' incarcerated, he recognised he was wrong.[10] He pleaded, 'I would be grateful if you could arrange some kind of course, that I can do where I can properly learn Islam and its teachings.' The debate goes on regarding whether Khan was feigning, but he chose to carry out his attack while set to attend a conference

---

[8] 'Beyond The Conversation: Context-Fluid Experiences and Augmented Cognition', *Boxes and Arrows*, 4 October 2016, available at: https://boxesandarrows.com/beyond-the-conversation-context-fluid-experiences-and-augmented-cognition/

[9] Operation Guava, 2012; London Bridge stabbing, 2019.

[10] 'Hundreds of former jihadis are set to be freed from jail. London terror attack show the risk', *CNN*, 1 December 2019, available at: https://edition.cnn.com/2019/12/01/uk/london-bridge-attack-analysis-gbr-intl/index.html

on violent offender rehabilitation.[11] This certainly may have been an expression of his frustration with the contextual and cultural circumstances that surrounded his reintegration.

Khan ultimately engaged in two programmes. While incarcerated, he completed, the UK's Healthy Identity Intervention Programme (HIIP), an untested, psychologically-informed intervention developed by a small team of psychologists, a probation officer and a Muslim Sheik in conjunction with an Interventions Unit, a group that has worked for decades to advance interventions for a range of offending behaviour (i.e. sexual offending and chemical dependence).[12] The programme seeks to construct new identities for extremism-related offenders while they are incarcerated, to address the lack of purpose, significance, and meaning and identity fusion that results when people find these needs met by extremist movements and ideologies.

The intervention is conducted in prison settings and on a one-on-one basis. So, the relationship between the inmate and interventionist is crucial to the process, and while it seeks to create a new individual identity through one-on-one dialogue, it does not connect to a real-world network and narrative, one that would permit programme participant's to have psycho-social needs met by an alternative group or movement that provides a similar sense of meaning, purpose and significance to that which extremists offer their

---

[11] 'Portrait of London Bridge Killer, in His Own Words', *The New York Times*, 5 December 2019, available at: https://www.nytimes.com/2019/12/05/world/europe/london-bridge-attack-extremist.html; 'How to rehabilitate a terrorist', *The Economist*, 5 December 2019, available at: https://www.economist.com/britain/2019/12/05/how-to-rehabilitate-a-terrorist

[12] Christopher Dean, 'The healthy identity intervention: the UK's development of a psychologically informed intervention to address extremist offending', in *Prisons, Terrorism and Extremism: Critical Issues in Management, Radicalisation and Reform*, ed. by Andrew Silke (Oxon, 2014)

adherents. It is one thing to talk about group belonging, and another to actually provide real-world alternatives.

After release, Khan also engaged in the UK's Desistance and Disengagement Programme, an initiative that 'provides a range of intensive, tailored interventions and practical support designed to tackle the drivers of radicalisation.'[13] Support could include mentoring, psychological support, as well as theological and ideological advice. It too, is conducted on a one-on-one basis and so results will only be as good as the interventionist. Is it possible this post-release engagement re-radicalised him?

I've met several convicted jihadists that were re-radicalised by well-intended imams and other interventionists attempting to teach some sort of 'true moderate Islam,' without the actual expertise necessary to assess when and how to discuss ideology, and the role it plays in formulating identity.[14] The problem is one of epistemology. Moderate imams may have studied a moderate interpretation of their religion, but that doesn't necessarily mean they have a thorough grasp of the salafi-jihadist worldview. Time and time again, I've been told stories of efforts to refute the jihadist theology, but that these imams never addressed the equally important political component that makes jihadism a holistic and powerful revolutionary counterculture. On the other side, I've met tens of Muslims that claimed to have left behind Bin Laden or Abu Bakr Al-Baghdadi's extremism, but continued to espouse belief in politicised Islam, 7th century shariah, conspiracy theory, antisemitism, Muslim superiority, and

---

[13] 'Fact sheet: Desistance and Disengagement Programme', *Home Office in the Media*, 5 November 2019, available at: https://homeofficemedia.blog.gov.uk/2019/11/05/fact-sheet-desistance-and-disengagement-programme/

[14] 'Sleeper Cells: Two Generations of American Jihad', *Parallel Networks*, 20 April 2017, available at: http://pnetworks.org/sleeper-cells-two-generations-of-american-jihad/

the like. And guess what? These views are prevalent in mosqued communities throughout the West. Nevertheless, when we talk deradicalisation, we often include falsely labelled 'moderate' imams that retain these views, even if they keep them private.

We might think of the difference between disengagement and deradicalisation in the same way we think of the distinctions between abstinence and recovery in substance abuse treatment. I was released from prison early, seemingly deradicalised, on 1 March 2015. I had cooperated with law enforcement but returned to an American society that offered no formal programming for terrorist offenders. After being outed as an FBI informant by the *Washington Post* a year later, I found a home at a D.C. think tank and went public as America's first former jihadist in August 2016.[15] My story was covered all over the press; I spoke on panels and at conferences; I had a second chance at life. Many called for scepticism, questioning the 'deradicalisation' narrative.[16] I fell apart. Soon thereafter, I relapsed on drugs for the first time in 15 years.[17] It

---

[15] 'The feds billed him as a threat to American freedom. Now they're paying him for help', *Washington Post*, 5 February 2016, available at: https://www.washingtonpost.com/local/public-safety/the-feds-billed-him-as-a-threat-to-american-freedom-now-theyre-paying-him-for-help/2016/02/04/32be460a-c6c5-11e5-a4aa-f25866ba0dc6_story.html; 'An extremist's path to academia – and fighting terrorism', *Public Broadcasting Service*, 29 August 2016, available at: https://www.pbs.org/newshour/show/extremists-path-academia-fighting-terrorism

[16] Terror 'Defector' Stories Hyped by Media Collapse Underneath the 'Deradicalization' Narrative', *PJ Media*, 16 March 2017, available at: https://pjmedia.com/homeland-security/patrick-poole/2017/03/16/terror-defector-stories-hyped-by-media-collapse-underneath-the-deradicalization-narrative-n95557

[17] 'Man who turned away from radical Islam arrested on drug, prostitution charges', *The Washington Post*, 25 January 2017, available at: https://www.washingtonpost.com/local/public-safety/man-who-turned-away-from-radical-islam-arrested-on-drug-prostitution-charges/2017/01/25/70a9627e-de7a-11e6-ad42-f3375f271c9c_story.html

seemed that deradicalisation simply entailed leaving the ideology. I didn't grasp that jihadism often serves as an opiate, numbing anxiety while providing an intoxicant that grants victimhood and portrays self-destruction as martyrdom. In a sense, society was fortunate. My blow-up occurred in the context of mingling with professionals. Under alternative circumstances, my relapse could have been a bomb or bullet.

The process of disengaging from deeply meaningful and embodied identities can be similar to a struggle against addiction, with continuing cognitive, emotional, and physiological responses that are involuntary, unwanted and triggered by environmental factors.[18] There is a lot we can learn from addiction therapy. Often substance abusers are mandated to complete addiction treatment. However, effective addiction-related programmes synthesise group and individual therapy. The mandated circumstances, however, permit a programme objective that departs from merely addressing the addict's personal needs.

While I was one of the most prominent jihadist recruiters, I worked as a substance abuse counsellor in Brooklyn, New York. The discrepancy between attitudes and behaviour expressed in individual versus group sessions allowed for an indicator of whether programme participants would effectively transition from abstinence to actual recovery. Often, in individual sessions, participants would detail personal ambitions, a desire to stop using and a realisation of the harm and havoc addiction inflicted. Yet, in group sessions it became clear that they still found the

---

[18] Pete Simi, Kathleen Blee, Matthew DeMichele and Steven Windisch, 'Addicted to Hate: Identity Residual among Former White Supremacists', *American Sociological Review*, 29 August 2017. Available at: https://www.dhs.gov/sites/default/files/publications/1003_OPSR_TP_Addicted-to-Hate_2017-508.pdf

counterculture of addiction amusing and need fulfilling. As they say in recovery, 'If nothing changes, nothing changes.' We remind addicts of the need to change people, places and things. It is another way of saying change your network, context and culture. When addicts enter 12-step programmes like Alcoholics or Narcotics Anonymous, they are encouraged to work with a sponsor, but the true support comes in attending meetings with the likeminded. New social bonds formulate and offer a new sense of purpose and belonging. Once one-on-one sessions are over, reintegrating terrorism-related offenders return to ofttimes isolated real-world settings. And as we also say in addiction therapy, 'An addict alone is an addict in bad company.'

Additionally, substance abuse programmes are not merely about treatment. They also include monitoring mechanisms. Addicts are required to submit urinalysis. Counsellors observe phenomenon, such as the discrepancies between attitude and behaviour in individual and group sessions, to identify relapse risk factors and prospects of feigning. Counsellors are required to report regularly to probation officers. There is, therefore, a fluid connection between criminal justice and community-based organisations. Similarly, we should change the goalposts of rehabilitation and reintegration programming for terrorism-related convicts so that they target disengagement but also focus on protecting the public. There may be no way to measure extremism through physiological assessment, such as urinalysis, but qualified interventionists can identify similar discrepancies when programme involvement puts participants in individual and group settings.

Deradicalisation, as a concept, is often used too lightly. We also need to think in terms of networks. Revolution Muslim, the organisation I cofounded, was connected to 15 terrorism cases and monitored on five continents.[19] By the time it was disbanded, my cohorts and I had set a template for online radicalisation that ISIS went on to master.[20] My deradicalisation began in Morocco sometime before my own arrest in 2011, but I am constantly reminded of the long-lasting ramifications. For example, Khuram Bhutt, one of the 2017 London Bridge killers, was a Revolution Muslim administrator back in 2010.[21] Usman Khan was part of a cell that planned to attack the London Stock Exchange, a cell I helped radicalise.[22] 'Shaykh' Abdullah Faisal, Revolution Muslim's chief imam, influenced Sudesh Amman, who carried out the other major recidivist attack in the UK on 2 February 2020, stabbing two in London just days after his release.[23]

There are others, but if we understood the ideology and identity that networks preserve over time, we'd be better able to assess the threat adherents to these networks pose after they are forcibly disengaged by arrest or other forms of involuntary intervention. Every time a member of an extremist organisation turns to violence, the coverage

[19] Jesse Morton and Mitchell Silber, 'NYPD vs. Revolution Muslim: The Inside Story of the Defeat of a Local Radicalization Hub', CTC Sentinel (New York, 2018). Available at: https://ctc.usma.edu/wp-content/uploads/2018/04/CTC-SENTINEL-042018-3.pdf

[20] Mitchell Silber and Jesse Morton, 'From Revolution Muslim to Islamic State: An Inside Look at the American Roots of ISIS' Virtual Caliphate', New America, 24 May 2018, available at: https://www.newamerica.org/international-security/reports/revolution-muslim-islamic-state/introduction/

[21] 'Meet the Former Extremist Who Flagged a London Attacker in 2015', The New York Times, 6 June 2017, available at: https://www.nytimes.com/video/world/europe/100000005147965/fbi-london-attacker-khuram-butt.html

[22] 'Stock Exchange plotters: Fantasists or a threat?', BBC News, 9 February 2012, available at: https://www.bbc.co.uk/news/uk-16953938

[23] 'Streatham terror attacker devoted to 'sheikh' who inspired London Bridge killer', The Times, 5 February 2020, available at: https://www.thetimes.co.uk/article/streatham-terror-attacker-devoted-to-sheikh-who-inspired-london-bridge-killer-lpd5wplnt

and scrutiny it warrants risks revitalising the movement, retaining its legacy and resonance.

I also agree with Aimen Dean that, 'The only way [jihadists] can demonstrate that they've renounced violent extremism is if they have sung like a canary and provided damaging intelligence on the networks that recruited them.' After I pled guilty, I had to undergo debriefing with the NYPD, FBI, MI6 and other agencies.[24] Soon into it, I faced a dilemma. Back in the SHU (solitary housing unit), another jihadist informed me of impending plots on the outside. To tell on a Muslim is tantamount to apostasy for jihadists, but I forwarded the information. It established trust, trust that I was actually altering my perspective, and, for me, further trust that they weren't waging war on Islam but simply protecting the public. When many of those Revolution Muslim influenced started turning up in Syria with ISIS, my input proved essential in tracking their nefarious endeavours. However, most terrorism-related offenders will not have actionable intelligence. Still, their willingness to engage in conversations with law enforcement can serve as testimony to their sincerity.

Over the past few years, the organisation I co-founded with the former director of intelligence at the NYPD has offered support to terrorism-related offenders around the English-speaking world, without any government involvement.[25] In the US, we face a similar dilemma. Since September 11,

---

[24] 'Leader of Revolution Muslim Pleads Guilty to Using Internet to Solicit Murder and Encourage Violent Extremism', *Washington Field Office*, 9 February 2012, available at: https://archives.fbi.gov/archives/washingtondc/press-releases/2012/leader-of-revolution-muslim-pleads-guilty-to-using-internet-to-solicit-murder-and-encourage-violent-extremism; https://www.investigativeproject.org/documents/case_docs/1904.pdf

[25] 'The Making – and Unmaking – of a Jihadist', *Wall Street Journal*, 4 May 2018, available at: https://www.wsj.com/articles/the-makingand-unmakingof-a-jihadist-1525472372; Morton and Silber, 'NYPD vs. Revolution Muslim', *Combating Terrorism Center* (2018)

2001, almost 900 people have been prosecuted for terrorism-related crimes. The federal inmate population currently includes over 500 domestic and international terrorists. While an overriding majority of terrorism-related cases since 9/11 have been jihadist in orientation, a review of federal prosecutions between 2001 and March 23, 2019 identified 268 right-wing extremists involved in crimes that appeared to meet the legal definition of terrorism. Over the next five years, nearly 25% of those incarcerated for jihadist offences will complete their terms of imprisonment.[26] We recognise that the risk is real, but also that former extremists, such as myself, can reform and might serve as the most effective interventionists, especially in the realm of identifying risks of relapse or feigning.

To rule deradicalisation out because a subset of those disengaged return to violence intensifies risk: elevating anti-Muslim bias, enhancing far-right wing recruitment, further stigmatizing terrorism-related offenders and increasing the likelihood that their disengagement will not evolve to full-blown deradicalisation. Our main focus is not merely on individual change through one-on-one mentorship, but in creating opportunities to engage in other programming. We've created a psycho-social support group comprised of former extremists, survivors of extremism, activists and academics dedicated to combating polarisation, hate and extremism.[27] Programme participants have written articles,

---

[26] 'America's Terrorism Problem Doesn't End with Prison – It Might Just Begin There', *Lawfare*, 17 June 2018. Available at: https://www.lawfareblog.com/americas-terrorism-problem-doesnt-end-prison%E2%80%94it-might-just-begin-there

[27] Jesse Morton and Mitchell D. Silber, 'When Terrorists Come Home: The Need for Rehabilitating and Reintegration America's Convicted Jihadists', *Counter Extremism Project* (2018). Available at: https://www.counterextremism.com/sites/default/files/CEP%20Report_When%20Terrorists%20Come%20Home_120618.pdf

presented their lived experience to public audiences, contributed to counter-messaging videos, podcasts and mainstream media pieces, helped to monitor online extremist activities and are supported by frequent group calls and private chat discussions.

In conclusion, scrapping the belief in deradicalisation is not an option. If we don't get disengagement and 'deradicalisation' right, we may face a similar wave of violence in America. However, unlike in Britain, we don't have any formal deradicalisation-oriented programme, either in prison or upon release.[28] If a single incident occurs in the US, the controversy won't be about whether what the government did was wrong, it will be about why they did nothing. As we are consumed with coverage of Covid-19, we would do well to continue advancing our ability to provide effective rehabilitation and reintegration for the terrorism-related offenders set to return to society. As we all should be able to see, the context, climate and culture are ripe.

---

[28] 'American's Terrorism Problem Doesn't End with Prison – It might Just Begin there', *Lawfare*, 17 June 2018. Available at: https://www.lawfareblog.com/americas-terrorism-problem-doesnt-end-prison%E2%80%94it-might-just-begin-there

Why we should treat released terrorists like sex offenders
Ian Acheson

In the countries of the United Kingdom, those imprisoned for terrorist or extremism related offences will be almost exclusively supervised in the community post-custody by agencies of the state. The majority of this supervision will take place following instructions first produced by HM Prison Service in 2014, 'Managing terrorist and extremist offenders in the community.' From December 2018, these instructions have been augmented by the Desistence and Disengagement programme (DDP) designed by the Home Office and updated specific guidance for probation staff for the assessment of offenders sentenced under the Terrorism Act. It appears that these disparate approaches were to be consolidated in a single 'Managing Extremism policy Framework' promised by HM Prison and Probation Service for March 2019. This document is either so confidential that the senior operational people I have spoken to haven't seen it – a bit of an own goal – or it doesn't yet exist. In the tortuously secretive convolutions of the current terrorist prisoner management world, the latter would not surprise me.

The 2014 instruction provides guidance and a rationale for managing extremism related offenders, 'through the gate,' requiring preparation by prisons and the National Probation Service who are responsible for the management of all high-risk terrorist and terrorist related offenders. The objective of the approach is:

> '...that those offenders who have committed offences of terrorism...or terrorism related offences or whose offences are linked to other forms of extremism, or who are vulnerable to engagement in forms of extremism are correctly identified, assessed and managed within offender management.'

The management of those at highest risk in the community will also involve other agencies such as the police, security services and selected statutory agencies.

The practical reality of managing a multi-agency relationship based on the sharing of sensitive security information cannot be overlooked and is highly relevant to the development of effective reintegration. Special arrangements for managing high risk/high harm individuals released from custody have been in place in England and Wales (with Scottish and Northern Irish variants) since 2000. These teams which involve police, probation and other 'responsible authorities' working together are known as 'Multi Agency Public Protection Arrangements' or MAPPA. By far the largest number of cases managed by MAPPA were and remain sex offenders or those who pose a risk in the community due to non-ideologically motivated dangerousness. This coupled with a dramatically smaller caseload means that specialist police and counter terrorism agencies with a culture of secrecy such as the police national counter terrorist command, SO15 and the security service, MI5, have had less time to develop trustful relationships with other partners.

A study ten years ago by the RAND Corporation into how well MAPPA functioned in managing terrorist offenders found examples of this:

'it's… like a micro version of MAPPA in the sense that the problems that we had when MAPPA first started about getting probation on board and working alongside probation and not just probation but other agencies, and the police, encouraging them to be more forthcoming with information… because people are very guarded initially.'

While there have been improvements and new joint units galore in the meantime, the statutory shotgun marriage of multiple agencies with widely differing organisational philosophies, hierarchies and objectives, working in different permutations at different points in the offenders journey through custody into the community remains highly problematic.

The absence of any bespoke predictive tool to identify the risk of terrorist reoffending is another important factor. There is a generic tool for all offenders – OaSys – but doubt exists about the effectiveness of this tool as a predictor of future risk because:

- Common criminogenic 'flags' may be absent. In other words, joblessness and anti-social behaviour may be absent in this cohort which would otherwise be predictors of future offending.

- Extremist offenders may have no prior convictions which is another important predictive factor in OaSys.

In fairness, these limitations have been recognised and OaSys is now supplemented by newer (though not independently assurance tested) extremism risk guidance and screening tools. However, the sense of a 'Heath Robinson' approach where standard risk management is retrofitted to meet the unique challenges of violent religion inspired fundamentalism persists.

Another highly relevant problem highlighted by the RAND report relates to the cultural 'dissonance' between professionals and extremist offenders. This was neatly summed up by a forensic psychiatrist working for the probation service:

> 'If I was to sit down with a terrorist, I just feel that the ability for that individual to relate to my experience and me to relate to theirs, it is far removed from any other offence type for me… the cultural differences somehow … make it hard.'

Finally, the motivation and commitment of the offender to co-operate with statutory authorities is problematic. There is a strong association between those who display or have acquired radical beliefs in custody and oppositional behaviour. An over emphasis on the importance of a collaborative approach seen in some current assessment tools and interventions while positive in theory could be less so in practice when dealing with some highly sophisticated and manipulative terrorist offenders adept at gaming the system and exploiting naivety.

It is unlikely that those terrorist offenders who leave custody with their ideology intact perceive their engagement with the state in a positive light. As one probation professional in the RAND study put it:

> 'One of the issues about this group is that for some of them, they have an anti-West standpoint and will not engage in any way because you're authority. So one of the things we're developing is a motivational engagement intervention which … doesn't talk about their offending in any way, just looks at what's important to them in their lives, and their issues in their lives and their life in the future.'

On the contrary, it is also quite possible that the positive 'disruption' caused by being engaged with professionally by someone from another culture could be beneficial as this Ministry of Justice professional put it:

'For someone who might not have had really any contact outside a fairly narrow group of Muslim people, to have someone from the hated group, and I'm not saying all our staff achieve this, but the best of our staff do... to form an alliance and form a relationship...just that, is very important in beginning to get people to question some of their assumptions around how they construct the world.'

Their successful reintegration would seem to depend ultimately on a careful blend of control and encouragement. It is unlikely that they regard the MAPPA system – dominated by understandable concerns of control and risk from state agencies – as acting in their interests. As unpalatable as this concern might seem for people who may have planned for, caused or facilitated horrific harm, it is one we must pay attention to in the design of an effective re-entry process for these offenders which keeps them – and us – safe. It is also worth dwelling on the impact of imprisonment itself as a motivating or demotivating factor for successful reintegration.

Our prison system is struggling in many ways to maintain basic levels of decency and control due to a combination of understaffing and overcrowding. Within this febrile environment the threat of radicalisation is growing. Insufficient staff, poorly trained and lacking confidence, have been unable to counter the spread of hateful ideologies pedalled by sophisticated and charismatic prisoners. Ungoverned spaces, taken over by gangs – some of these ideologically motivated – flourish. A lack of training, supervision and proper management means that prison Imams who ought to be front and centre in the battle to counter extremism have neither the tools nor sometimes the will to be effective. Moreover, the offending behaviour tools which have been created to help extremists tackle their identity-based offending are at best generic and primitive and at worst able to be manipulated by offenders to feign disengagement. The lack of engagement by extremist offenders was starkly revealed in a Sky News investigation in November 2016. It found that of the 583 people given custodial sentences for terrorism since September 2001, almost 75% (418) had been released from custody. It found that 2/3 of those imprisoned refused to engage with deradicalisation programmes available then.

Although these figures include those given short sentences and may well also reflect the availability and suitability of programmes, it gives a disturbing shape to the numbers of released extremists who may not have had their offending behaviour challenged in any meaningful way.

Finally, the lack of a coherent strategy to understand the threat of extremism properly or take action against it has meant that in some instances, prisons have become incubators for extremism allowing radicalisers and prisoners vulnerable to hateful and anti-British ideas relatively free access to each other. While these deficiencies are being slowly tackled, the fact remains that a permissive environment for extremist ideas has been allowed to grow unchecked and this will have a direct impact on the mindset, motivation and values of some of those imprisoned for extremism or terrorist related offences.

It also creates a new and dangerous subset of risky offenders – those who may have been imprisoned for 'ordinary' offences who are emerging after relatively short periods of custody having been radicalised by subversive elements in custody. The dangers posed by these offenders are still poorly understood – in part because the systems which may identify them as being at risk have failed or because they have completed their sentences entirely 'below the radar' in lower security prisons with neither the capacity nor capability to pick up their offending. Any effective re-integration process can only work if those at risk of continuing or new extremist offending are picked up and communication goes 'through the gate' to agencies, ahead of the offender's release. In summary, the challenges attached to extremist offenders emerging from our criminal justice system are formidable in terms of their successful re-entry into the community. Their past and future offending has been shaped by an experience unlikely to have been positive with few meaningful opportunities to explore other forms of being.

This depressing reality is underlined by the paucity of effective treatment in custody for those convicted of extremist offences. There is also some concern that this, coupled with more punitive sentencing for those offenders peripheral to actual terrorist planning, might actually increase their dangerousness in custody and on release. The House of Commons Justice select committee reported on proposals to increase sentences for terrorist offenders. The committee had sought views from the Parole Board who said: 'In the Board's assessment, there are concerns that increasing the penalties for less serious offenders will result in them becoming more likely to commit terrorist acts when they are released.'

The Board goes on to observe:

> 'Most of the rest of Europe is devising interventions in the community to deradicalise less serious offenders. These programmes are more likely to be successful in the community than in prison where the influence of extremist inmates is likely to be stronger'.

These comments plainly illustrate the value and importance of community-based interventions to reintegrate offenders after custody. It will continue to be shaped by official power which controls, curtails and supervises freedom. This power will be applied differentially according to risk algorithms which are not designed specifically for them and by people largely culturally disconnected from their experience.

The imperative to manage risky extremists through the gate and into the community is increased by the emergency Sentencing Bill passed in the light of twin attacks perpetrated by released terrorists either side of Christmas 2019 that underlined serious deficiencies in the way multi-agency could and did manage harm. In particular, Usman Khan's murderous rampage while a guest at an event to celebrate the work of a rehabilitation charity he was helped by illustrated just how broken the terrorist risk management system had become. The later attack in Streatham by Sudesh Amman, automatically released from custody but considered still so dangerous he was shadowed by armed officers also served to illustrate the impotence of the law and undermined public confidence. Clearly not enough was being done to protect the public from those still motivated to cause harm in the name of ideology after release.

While the needs of public protection must always be paramount, successful long-term reintegration must be the policy goal for terrorist offenders to enable them to have the best shot at disengaging from their hateful and destructive worldview. The genuinely recanting terrorist is a potent and valuable prize in a liberal democracy. In this respect, the resettlement needs of our 220 odd extremist offenders currently in custody will be as diverse as the factors which led them into their offending. They may experience feelings of shame, alienation and dislocation unique to their offence profile. Their prospects for employment, already parlous in this post-Covid world, will be likely even more constrained than those of 'ordinary decent criminals.' Their prospects for desistence and disengagement will depend on a response that meets these variables and allows them to buy into a process which calls on them, essentially, to jettison what may be deeply rooted beliefs and behaviours

What would a new model for reintegration look like and how could it be delivered? What role could faith communities play in this delivery? Circles of Support and Accountability (CoSA) was established in Ontario, Canada, in 1994 by a Mennonite pastor who was looking for ways to prevent a serial sex offender from victimising more people.

He and some parishioners formed a support 'circle' around the offender. He did not re-offend. An international movement has emerged from this experiment which now supports the safe re-integration of hundreds of high-risk sex-offenders worldwide. CoSA in the UK was set up by the Quakers in 2002.

The CoSA model was based on projects which had been running in Canada for a number of years that had supported the safe integration of high risk and high profile sexual offenders in local communities. 'Circles' consist of four to six local volunteers and one sexual offender who has recently been released from custody and is subject to statutory supervision on licence. The volunteers are known as 'Lay Members' of the Circle, whilst the sexual offender is referred to as the 'Core Member'.

The volunteers regularly meet with the Core Member and aim to provide social and practical support to reduce the risk of social isolation, to monitor their actions to ensure the local community is safe, and to hold them accountable for their actions and participation in treatment programmes.

The aim is to reintegrate the Core Member safely into his/her community and to reduce their risk of re-offending.

The UK organisation has established an umbrella group, Circles UK, which sets standards for volunteer recruitment, training and supervision. Participation is based on a level of acceptance by the offender that s/he requires assistance and wants to change. The delivery is complementary to statutory service supervision which is a mandatory feature of all high risk/high harm offenders in this category. The model is conceptualised as two concentric rings of support around an offender, the inner ring around the 'core' – the offender – consists of volunteer mentors who monitor and support the offender day-to-day. The outer rings consist of professionals including probation, psychology and police who deal with enforcement and treatment. The process has been subject to validation in the United States, Canada and the United Kingdom. In all studies rates of recidivism and parole violations were lower than for individuals in control groups that did not participate. There are distinct similarities between ideologically motivated offenders and those who commit sexual offences in terms of their criminogenic development and needs:

- Both groups are regarded as 'taboo' offenders;

- Dehumanisation of others is a pre-requisite;

- Notions of power and control are dominant;

- Both may experience isolation and alienation in prison;

- Both are routinely subject to stringent controls on release into the community and extended periods of supervision through MAPPA;

- Both may encounter particular forms of shame and

shunning in the community and within the family environment that are risk factors for repeat offending;

- Both are likely to encounter social isolation;

- Both will have particular difficulty in obtaining housing and employment.

The Circles concept combines the theoretical frameworks of Restorative Justice (RJ) and the Good Lives Model (GLM). Restorative Justice is based on remorse, repair and reconciliation. It can involve communication between the perpetrator and victim where the perpetrator takes responsibility for their actions and attempts some form of repair within his means.

The Good Lives Model is predicated on the idea that, with assistance, offenders can develop life plans which are incompatible with future offending. The Good Lives Model (GLM) is a framework of offender rehabilitation which, given its holistic nature, addresses the limitations of the traditional risk management approach. The GLM has been adopted as a grounding theoretical framework by several sex offender treatment programmes internationally and is now being applied successfully in a case management setting for other offenders including violent extremists. The GLM is a strengths-based approach to offender rehabilitation and is therefore premised on the idea that we need to build capabilities and strengths in people, in order to reduce their risk of reoffending. It recognises that reducing criminological needs is a necessary, but not a sufficient, condition, for effective interventions. GLM assumes that offenders, like all humans, value certain states of mind, personal characteristics, and experiences, which are defined as 'primary goods'. These are:

1. Life (including healthy living and functioning)

2. Knowledge (how well informed one feels about things that are important to them)

3. Excellence in play (hobbies and recreational pursuits)

4. Excellence in work (including mastery experiences)

5. Excellence in agency (autonomy, power and self-directedness)

6. Inner peace (freedom from emotional turmoil and stress)

7. Relatedness (including intimate, romantic, and familial relationships)

8. Community (connection to wider social groups)

9. Spirituality (in the broad sense of finding meaning and purpose in life)

10. Pleasure (feeling good in the here and now)

11. Creativity (expressing oneself through alternative forms).

Would the elements of this approach work with ideologically motivated offenders? CoSA has not been applied to any other offender group but this is not because it has been deemed incompatible, it is more a reflection of professional focus and competence. The Head of Policy at Circles UK has indicated that in principle there is no conceptual reason why this approach could not be employed with ideologically motivated offenders.

Moreover, a CoSA rooted approach could be delivered through faith groups where it is appropriate. CoSA emerged from such a group and in the UK started life through the Quakers. While it has a secular, humanist approach now, the process seems equally compatible with delivery from a Mosque or Church.

Indeed, for the predominant ideological offender cohort – Islamist extremists – this might be the only approach which would gain acceptance and traction with the offender. There are obvious and deep challenges associated with such an approach. In the first instance, this sort of intervention would need to be branded entirely separately from CoSA. The stigma of sexual offending transcends most ideologies and none. Association with a concept solely associated with sexual violence could make the concept unworkable.

Moreover, identifying, attracting, training and supervising 'civilian' mentors working closely with people convicted of terrorism offences and who live in the same community is problematic. There would necessarily need to be security clearance for individuals working in close proximity with such offenders. The available evidence suggests that long-term engagement provides the key to desistence and eventual disengagement from terrorism. Conditioning and manipulation are also risk factors. Finally, the distinction between state supervision and community engagement would require very careful management. There must be a two-way relationship to protect public safety and make efficient use of resources. With this offender group, however, building a relationship of trust with someone who offends in opposition to the state is key to success. This will be a difficult circle to square.

These difficulties are not insurmountable. There are obvious and large gains in mobilising the talent in communities to be part of the solution to violent extremism. The experience of Northern Ireland teaches us that, whatever the security response, extremism can survive unless and until communities are brought into the fold as partners against violence. In Great Britain, recent experience of Islamist extremism terrorist outrages has brought with it unfair stigmatisation of whole communities. By participating in such a programme, Muslim communities could counter some of this misplaced and undeserved suspicion.

Community interaction with ideologically inspired offenders is also likely to make compliance and desistence more likely to succeed as the burden is shared between the state and the community as with many jurisdictions in Europe. Behaviours demonstrated by people from the same heritage who demonstrate empathy and pro-social ways of being who model 'good lives' are more likely to take root in the offender than those imposed remotely by criminal justice professionals concerned only with risk.

So how might the CoSA process operate in practice in the Muslim community? Here is a simple and illustrative 'worked example.' The 'Sunnah' (Arabic for 'path') network:

Conviction: Saafir, 19, is sentenced to 3 years in prison under Terrorism Act 2006 legislation for Preparation of Terrorist Acts. This is the low end of the scale.

Identification: During his custody in a young adult prison establishment he is identified by the inreach team as suitable for the 'Sunnah' support network on release. Saafir's family is involved in this decision.

Engagement: The inreach team liaise with the MAPPA team in Saafir's community to set up a circle of support for him on release. A comprehensive needs assessment is made. MAPPA Co-ordination liaises with the Sunnah lead, the Imam of Saafir's local Mosque who will be co-ordinating the community support. Participation in the programme is made a licence condition for Saafir's release. The Imam is asked to sit on the local MAPPA strategic board as a lay advisor.

Community response: Saafir is released from custody. His supervision is managed by MAPPA in close conjunction with the Sunnah lead. He is collected from custody by his lead mentor.

Desistence: Sunnah programme volunteer mentors meet regularly with Saafir. His community support and supervision programme is a tailored combination of theological instruction and exposure to diverse cultures, communities and people. Saafir visits a Synagogue and joins a local multi-ethnic football team. Sunnah mentors help Saafir set up a life plan which meets his ambition to work for himself.

Disengagement: MAPPA supervision formally ends as Saafir's licence expires. Saafir continues to receive close voluntary support from the Sunnah programme. Saafir agrees to become part of the Sunnah team and speaks in schools and in his Mosque about the benefits of the programme. This is, of course, a stylised description with a successful outcome but it conveys a sense of what could be possible in terms of community safety and reintegration if such a process existed.

We cannot let the burden of reintegration fall on the state agencies, imperfectly configured as they are. While involvement of those protective services is essential for public protection it is a necessary but insufficient response to the challenge of helping extremists slough off their terrorist identity and safeguarding us from long term harm. Bringing local communities into the equation as partners, separate from but complimentary to the control agencies security approach in the way described above could be a game changer. Recent research on the Prevent programme by the Crest advisory group gives the lie to lazy and dangerous assumptions about British Muslims and terrorism. Contrary to the stereotypical prejudice, British Muslims broadly support our counter terrorism approach. They ought to be full partners in our national security and the adaptation of the Circles approach set out above could be the bold and imaginative solution we are looking for to unite our community in an all-out effort to defeat violent extremism and prevent the next generation of offenders from ruining more lives. That's a prize worth taking some risks for.

Exit from extremist groups and reintegration: bringing evidence into policy
Julia Ruschenko

Introduction

On 29 November 2019, Usman Khan, armed with two knives, carried out an attack on a prisoner rehabilitation event in the London Bridge area, killing two and injuring three.[1] A few months later, Sudesh Amman stabbed two people in south London.[2] Both offenders had been released from prison half-way through their sentence through the automatic release scheme, having served only half of their sentences. Moreover, Usman Khan had completed the Healthy Identity Intervention Programme behind the bars and had participated in the mandatory Disengagement and Desistance programme post-release, and was deemed to be rehabilitated.[3] These attacks coupled with the background of perpetrators have brought to the fore the discussion around recidivism and reliability of existing risk assessments. To what extent can we have an informed understanding of whether a person no longer poses a risk to public? How can we ensure that terrorism-related offenders who had

---

[1] 'London Bridge: Family of Usman Khan 'shocked' by attack', *BBC News*, 3 December 2019, available at: https://www.bbc.co.uk/news/uk-50647972

[2] 'Streatham attacker named as Sudesh Amman', *BBC News*, 3 February 2020, available at: https://www.bbc.co.uk/news/uk-51351844

[3] 'London Bridge: Usman Khan completed rehabilitation scheme', *BBC News*, 4 December 2020, available at: https://www.bbc.co.uk/news/uk-50653191

completed deradicalisation programmes have given up on pursuing political violence? Finally, how can we measure the success of the violent extremism (VE)-related treatments?

Recent quantitative data indicates that ideological offenders are at an increased risk of recidivism in comparison to common criminality.[4] Although in February 2020, the UK government introduced emergency legislation blocking 50 jailed extremists from being released earlier, the issue of risk management of violent extremist offenders – both in custody and post-release – remains one of the most important security concerns in the context of combating radicalisation.[5] Risk management consists of strategies to prevent recidivism and to ensure that violent extremists do not pose a threat to society in terms of either new attacks or recruiting new followers. Rehabilitation programmes, interventions and risk assessments are part of the risk management process aimed at facilitating exit from radical environments and reintegration of extremist offenders into the community.

This chapter discusses lessons learned from criminology and desistance literature that could be applied to exit and reintegration of violent extremist offenders focusing on factors and conditions that contribute to this process. It also examines current challenges and barriers to rehabilitation programmes and treatments, including a potential for measuring efficacy of interventions.

---

[4] Badi Hasisi, Tomer Carmel, David Weisburd and Michael Wolfowicz, 'Crime and Terror: Examining Criminal Risk Factors for Terrorist Recidivism', *Journal of Quantitative Criminology* (2019). Available at: https://doi.org/10.1007/s10940-019-09415-y

[5] 'End to automatic early release of terrorists', *Ministry of Justice*, 11 February 2020. Available at: https://www.gov.uk/government/news/end-to-automatic-early-release-of-terrorists

Current challenges of rehabilitation programmes: evidence or political considerations?

A considerable part of the literature has explored the evidence-based approach of dealing with extremists and advocated for an empirical testing of counter terrorism interventions.[6] In practice, science-backed strategies are under-represented among the existing methods of combating radicalisation. The RNR model (risk, needs and responsivity) is currently the most commonly accepted evidenced-based model of offender risk assessment and rehabilitation. It is based on three principles:

(a) the level of treatment should be commensurate with the level of risk;

(b) the interventions should tackle offenders' criminogenic needs;[7]

(c) rehabilitation programmes should be tailored to offenders' personal circumstances, including their age, gender, race.[8]

---

[6] Cynthia Lum, Leslie W Kennedy, Alison Sherley, 'Is counter-terrorism policy evidence-based? What works, what harms, and what is unknown', *Psicothema* vol 20 (1) 2008. Available at: http://www.psicothema.com/PDF/3426.pdf; Tinka Veldhuis, 'Designing Rehabilitation and Reintegration Programmes for Violent Extremist Offenders: A Realist Approach', *International Centre for Counter-Terrorism*, March 2012. Available at: https://www.icct.nl/download/file/ICCT-Veldhuis-Designing-Rehabilitation-Reintegration-Programmes-March-2012.pdf; M. Herzog-Evans and M. Benbouriche, *Evidence-Based Work with Violent Extremists. International Implications of French Terrorist Attacks and Responses* (Lexington Books, Maryland, 2019)

[7] The need principle differentiates between criminogenic and non-criminogenic needs. The former are dynamic attributes that are directly associated with the likelihood of reoffending, whereas the latter are not directly linked to the probability of recidivism.

[8] Donald Andrews and James Bonta, 'Classification for Effective Rehabilitation: Rediscovering Psychology', *Criminal Justice and Behaviour*, Vol 17 (1) 1990. Available at: https://doi.org/10.1177/0093854890017001004

However, the widely accepted RNR model has not been tested on violent extremists, and it is possible to assume that different backgrounds of the ideologically-motivated individuals will require VE-specific assessment tools.

Although there is a consensus among the academic community that counter terrorism policy should be guided by research findings, the overview of deradicalisation programmes across jurisdictions suggests that policies continue being guided by the political considerations rather than being informed by the 'what works' approach.[9] On the one hand, it might be considered as negligence. On the other hand, some policies appear to be more appealing in terms of public acceptance or seem to be a better fit for a certain socio-cultural context. For example, the Saudi focus on repudiation of the doctrine of *takfir* and re-education of religious aspects is well-suited for the country's ideological framework. The notable features of the Indonesian approach to stamping out Islamism are based on the premise that radicals will only listen to radicals and that the only way to change the idea that the government is un-Islamic is through providing social and monetary services.[10] While there is a considerable debate regarding efficacy of these approaches (for example, the Saudi model has consistently been receiving positive evaluations with the success rate around 90% which some claim could be exaggerated), none of them were empirically tested and are not based on evidence.

However, an evidence-based approach is not always a silver bullet as policy transfer can lead to policy failure if best practices are taken from a completely different sociocultural

---

[9] Brigitte Nacos, *Terrorism and Counterterrorism* (New York, Routledge, 2016)

[10] Kristen E. Schulze, 'Indonesia's Approach to Jihadist Deradicalization', *CTC Sentinel* Vol. 1 (8) 2008. Available at: https://ctc.usma.edu/wp-content/uploads/2010/06/Vol1Iss8-Art3.pdf

and legal tradition. The conventional approaches to rehabilitation used in Europe will not necessarily work in the Israeli context, as security prisoners will eventually come back to the highly radicalising environment post-release. Likewise, the Saudi focus on religious re-education and ideological foundations of Islam might be frowned upon in secular countries. Furthermore, terrorism research, unlike any other crime-related topic, has always been hamstrung by the low samples coupled with the difficulties of access to informants. The latter is exacerbated by the slow rates of the desistance and disengagement process, and these complexities become even more pronounced when experts attempt to devise deradicalisation techniques or treatments.[11]

Exit and reintegration strategies: learning from the desistance literature

Despite decades of research on radicalisation, the process of leaving violent extremist organisations and causes is not well understood, and the facilitation of exit and reintegration stages remains a daunting task. At the same time, a number of important studies have been carried out on the process of disengaging from criminal organisations, cults and clandestine religious movements whose membership rules and recruitment strategies resemble those of violent extremist groups. Criminologists and sociologists have previously examined how deviant individuals, including alcoholics and drug addicts, rebuild their identities while disassociating from the former social milieu. Understanding what needs should be met for individuals to exit anti-social

---

[11] Liesbeth van der Heide and Robbert Huurman, 'Suburban Bliss or Disillusionment – Why Do Terrorists Quit?', *Journal for Deradicalization* No. 8 2016. Available at: https://journals.sfu.ca/jd/index.php/jd/article/view/64

movements without returning to the same environment is crucial while devising deradicalisation strategies.

Desistance literature has been rapidly developing since 1970s and 1980s. Drawing on a wide range of data from the United States, Fuchs Ebaugh (1988) offers an examination of people's motivations to leave identities that were once central to their lives.[12] After she herself broke away from the lifestyle of a Catholic nun in the 1970s, she has interviewed hundreds of individuals who had undergone drastic personal and professional changes or had left highly stigmatising roles (e.g., alcoholics, prostitutes or prisoners). Ebaugh argues that transition and change occur following four stages: 1) first doubts; 2) seeking alternatives; 3) turning points; 4) creating the ex-role. A decade later Månsson and Hedlin (1999) studied how women leave prostitution in Sweden and concluded that certain events facilitate their exit from sex industry: 1) eye-opening events; 2) traumatic events; 3) positive life events such as getting married or having a child.[13]

A review of existing exit strategies from political violence suggests that feelings of disillusionment and doubt play an important role in leaving violent extremist groups as 'push factors'. Barelle's interviews with 22 extremists in Australia confirm that the most powerful force that leads to leaving an extremist group is a feeling of disillusionment, particularly disillusionment with group leaders or its members.[14] In a

---

[12] Helen Rose Fuchs Ebaugh, *Becoming an ex: The process of role exit* (Chicago, 1988)

[13] S-A. Månsson and U-C. Hedin, 'Breaking the Matthew effect – on women leaving prostitution', *International Journal of Social Welfare*, vol 8 (1999). Available at: https://doi.org/10.1111/1468-2397.00063

[14] Kate Barrelle, 'Pro-integration: disengagement from and life after extremism', *Behavioral Sciences of Terrorism and Political Aggression*, vol 7 (2015). Available at: https://doi.org/10.1080/19434472.2014.988165

similar vein, an earlier research carried out by Bjørgo and Horgan's indicates that push factors of leaving a group are linked to either social sanctions or disillusionment.[15] Heide and Huurman (2016) interviewed twenty-seven ISIS-affiliated former foreign fighters who returned from Iraq and concluded that one of the reasons of their disaffection was excessive violence used by the group and disagreement over ISIS' tactics and methods.[16]

However, pinpointing what mechanisms lead to the exit from extremist organisations and removing external barriers to exiting do not suffice for developing an efficient rehabilitation strategy. Besides factors that facilitate exit it is important to understand what factors prevent returning to the same ideology and previous networks. There have previously been cases of relapse among extremist offenders who have seemingly deradicalised only to go back to their extremist surrounding. Bouchra Abouallal and Tatiana Wielandt, Belgian ISIS wives, moved to Syria to join their husbands in 2012. Having experienced the dangers and chaos of civil war, both women decided to come back to the safety of Europe. A few years later, being disappointed with their life in Belgium and the police scrutiny, they paid smugglers to return to Syria.[17]

It appears that certain conditions are crucial to ensure the individuals do not relapse into offending as in the latter case, regardless of the nature of a criminal or deviant behaviour.

---

[15] Tore Bjørgo and John Horgan, *Leaving Terrorism Behind: Individual and Collective Disengagement* (London, 2009)

[16] Heide and Huurman, 'Suburban Bliss or Disillusionment', *Journal for Deradicalization*. Available at: https://journals.sfu.ca/jd/index.php/jd/article/view/64

[17] Anne Speckhard, 'An ISIS Bride on the Run', *International Center for the Study of Violent Extremism*, 22 October 2019. Available at: https://www.icsve.org/an-isis-bride-on-the-run/

It is argued that supportive relationships, formal services, employment and a psychological readiness to change are pre-conditions required to ensure that women who had left sex industry maintain lives without engaging in sex work.[18] White and Kurtz (2006) and Maruna (2001) confirm that supportive social networks, a personal motivation and a secure employment are among circumstances that facilitate cessation of drug abuse among former addicts and help maintaining drug-free lifestyle.[19] Besides the latter, it is suggested that age contributes to desistance as offenders 'age out of crime, with a sheer passage of time'.[20] Finally, desistance is linked to the agency of the offender, and their own decisions and desires.[21]

Terrorist and criminal offenders have historically been considered as two separate categories of perpetrators. However, the crime-terror nexus research has challenged this notion proving that there is a significant overlap between the two, and many terrorists have previously had criminal histories for non-ideological crimes.[22] What conclusions

---

[18] Kristine E. Hickle, *Getting out: A Qualitative Exploration of the Exiting Experience Among Former Sex Workers and Adult Sex Trafficking Victims*, Arizona State University (2014). Available at: https://repository.asu.edu/attachments/134784/content/Hickle_asu_0010E_13637.pdf

[19] William White and Ernest Kurtz, *Recovery: Linking Addiction Treatment & Communities of Recovery: A Primer for Addiction Counselors and Recovery Coaches* (Pittsburgh, PA, 2006). Available at: http://www.williamwhitepapers.com/pr/2006RecoveryLinkageMonograph.pdf; Shadd Maruna, *Making good: How ex-convicts reform and reclaim their lives* (American Psychological Association, Washington DC, 2001)

[20] Maruna, *Making Good*, p. 27.

[21] Stephen Farrall, Anthony Bottoms and Joanna Shapland, 'Social Structures and desistance from crime', *European Journal of Crimonology*, 2010, vol 7 (6). Available at: https://doi.org/10.1177/1477370810376574

[22] Alexander Kupatadze and Javier Argomaniz, 'Introduction to Special Issue – Understanding and conceptualizing European jihadists: Criminal extremists or both?', *European Journal of Criminology*, vol 16 (3) 2019. Available at: https://doi.org/10.1177/1477370819829971; Rajan Basra and Peter R. Neumann, 'Crime as Jihad: Developments in the Crime-Terror Nexus in Europe', *CTC Sentinel*, vol 10 (9) October 2017. Available at: https://ctc.usma.edu/crime-as-jihad-developments-in-the-crime-terror-nexus-in-europe/

for violent extremism-related interventions in the United Kingdom can we draw based on the abovementioned desistance theories? Assuming that 'occurrence of critical incidents are necessary ingredients' for exit, it is possible to extrapolate this logic to the dynamics of exiting extremist groups.[23] Just like the situations of cognitive opening that 'renders an individual more receptive to the possibility of alternative views and perspectives' are used by Islamist groups to recruit new followers, similar techniques should be included while devising rehabilitation interventions.[24] Considering a trend of younger people being sentenced for terrorism offences in the UK, the age-crime curve suggested by Maruna will most likely not apply to them in the near future. Therefore, it is important to ensure that other factors, particularly social connections and career prospects, are addressed while devising rehabilitation interventions for the individuals released from prisons. How strong are their social bonds outside the extremist circles? How likely will they get a stable and satisfying employment? These are the questions for forensic psychologists and probation workers that would be helpful to address while developing risk assessments and treatments.

Although the desistance literature offers useful insights into the factors that facilitate exit from extremist groups, it has some limitations when applied to political offenders. While attachment to family and commitment to social norms are generally positively associated with reduction in offending, these protective factors do not always apply to political violence as extremism often spreads through

---

[23] Månsson and Hedin, 'Breaking the Matthew', *International Journal of Social Welfare*, (1999) p. 72. Available at: https://doi.org/10.1111/1468-2397.00063

[24] Quintan Wiktorowicz, *Radical Islam Rising: Muslim Extremism in the West* (Maryland, 2005), p. 20.

kinship networks, and spouses can be encouraging offending behaviour. There have been numerous cases of families traveling to conflict zones together and individuals recruiting family members. Another limitation is that the desistance scholarship overlooks any ideological influence as it has mostly focused on either anti-social habits or profit-oriented activities, and tackling ideological indoctrination while offering targeted alternative narratives for extremist offenders should be of a paramount importance for any successful rehabilitation strategy.

Success and failures: measuring efficacy of interventions

While assessing any social intervention, 'success' is a contested concept as it depends on the overarching theoretical framework and the impact a certain policy is designed to have. These aspects are meant to be clearly defined while formulating an intervention. Unlike the interpretivist paradigm, the realist approach maintains that it is impossible to understand what works in social interventions without establishing causal relationships and paying attention to the underlying mechanisms coupled with their contexts.[25] In other words, what works in one context might not work in another context, and policy transfer could be problematic.

The task of evaluating counter terrorism interventions is plagued with the same methodological complexities as the rehabilitation strategies that address common criminality. Galucci and Feddes argue that current assessments of interventions are mostly of an anecdotal nature with

---

[25] Ray Pawson, Trisha Greenhalgh, Gill Harvey and Kieran Walshe, 'Realist review – a new method of systematic review designed for complex policy interventions', *Journal of Health Services Research & Policy*, 2005, vol 10 (1). Available at: https://doi.org/10.1258/1355819054308530

no systematic evaluation strategy.[26] Herzog-Evans and Benbouriche maintain that there are no empirically validated assessment models, and the previously mentioned RNR model is not fit for purpose.[27] The process of deradicalisation consists of both disengagement and desistance as a result of behavioural and cognitive changes. Reflecting on the questions raised in the introduction, it is not clear how these processes take place and if a sudden relapse in terms of maintaining contact with the group or being committed to the same cause without any violent behaviour means that deradicalisation has failed. For example, Bottoms and Shapland argue that a possible relapse does not necessarily signify a full return to offending.[28] Furthermore, experts still question what percentage of recidivism is considered as a low one and whether individuals who have disengaged but not desisted can be successfully reintegrated into the society.[29]

Most literature on recidivism draws on the results reported from the rehabilitation programmes but their accuracy could be misleading. Hasisi et al. (2019) draws attention to the fact that some features of the data collection

---

[26] Allard R. Feddes and Marcello Gallucci, 'A Literature Review on Methodology used in Evaluating Effects of Preventative and De-radicalisation Interventions', *Journal for Deradicalization* (5) 2015. Available at: https://journals.sfu.ca/jd/index.php/jd/article/view/33

[27] Martine Herzog-Evans and Massil Benbouriche, *Evidence-Based Work with Violent Extremists: International Implications of French Terrorist Attacks and Responses* (Lexington Books, London: 2019)

[28] Joanna Shapland and Anthony Bottoms, 'Reflections on social values, offending and desistance among young adult recidivists', *Punishment & Society* vol 13 (3) 2011. Available at: https://doi.org/10.1177/1462474511404334

[29] Neil Ferguson, 'Disengaging from Terrorism: A Northern Irish Experience', *Journal for Deradicalization* 6 (2016). Available at: https://journals.sfu.ca/jd/index.php/jd/article/view/41; Andrew Silke, 'Terrorists and Extremists in Prison: Psychological Issues in Management and Reform', in Andrew Silke (Ed.), *The Pschyology of Counter Terrorism* (Routledge, London: 2011) pp. 123-34.

are obstacles to any reliable measurements: most evaluations focus on the 'treated' offenders (i.e. the so-called graduates of the programmes) and any published or announced results lack a longitudinal perspective as they are usually based on short periods of observation time (e.g. two years) resulting in skewed data.[30]

Conclusion and recommendations

Although the body of academic literature on radicalisation is extensive, a comprehensive understanding of how people exit the extremist movements and how to measure efficacy of rehabilitation programmes is lacking. At the same time, criminology and desistance literature offer a number of suggestions on how to facilitate exit from extremist groups and their further reintegration by anticipating problems that can lead to relapse. Drawing on the existing research on desistance, it is evident that the process of exiting a deviant group is linked to external factors such as social capital and financial stability. While the Saudi and Indonesian rehabilitation strategies have focused on both factors, to what extent have the European governments addressed the latter while dealing with former extremists (at least as part of the risk assessment models) is not clear. Alongside the internal and psychological factors already included in the ERG 22+[31] (i.e. 22 factors such as identity, mental health, dominance, status, threat, grievances included under three clusters of engagement, intent and culpability), a risk assessment model used in England and Wales, more attention should

---

[30] Badi Hasisi, Tomer Carmel, David Weisburd and Michael Wofowicz, 'Crime and Terror: Examining Criminal Risk Factors for Terrorist Recidivism', *Journal of Quantitative Criminology* (2019). Available at: https://doi.org/10.1007/s10940-019-09415-y

[31] ERG 22+ (Extremism Risk Guidelines) is a risk assessment tool used in the UK to measure the vulnerabilities among extremism-related offenders.

be paid to the social context, or the quality of productive social connections and career opportunities that are known to facilitate reintegration.

Returning to the idea of the importance of evidence for policy, cooperation with the private sector should be taking place beyond the content-related exchange expanding into the realm of the ideas. The government should consider using the practices of tech companies known for their emphasis on the data-driven approach to decision-making. Besides legislative changes, it is important to continue reviewing the existing deradicalisation approaches in line with the new data, and the adjustments should reflect the emerging trends of radicalisation, including the female involvement in terrorism and the young age of the terrorists. Most of the widely quoted studies on rehabilitation and recidivism worldwide have specifically focused on male offenders overlooking the amplifying voice of women as followers, recruiters and supporters of terrorism.

While it is tempting to design a quantitative assessment of counter extremism interventions to measure efficacy of treatments, complexities of any measurement or KPI regarding outcomes of deradicalisation are related to the following limitations: a non-linear process of desistance, sudden relapses if criminogenic and non-criminogenic needs have not been addressed in the long term, and selection bias if interventions are voluntary. Another point to consider is what criterion to use as a 'failure' of exit and reintegration: while incarceration and conviction are obvious indicators of the latter, maintaining affiliation with the organisation or showing interest in the same ideology are more controversial 'red flags'.

Tricked into terror?
Liam Duffy

In 2005, French television screened a documentary on the country's burgeoning domestic jihadist movement. In it, a young man once interested in rapping and chasing girls transforms into a would-be holy warrior, training for jihad in Paris' Buttes-Chaumont Park. A social worker who had exchanged correspondence with the now imprisoned young man explains how his prison sentence had shown him the error of his ways: 'He understood that he had been tricked and sucked into something that he himself didn't control or understand.'[1]

Ten years later that same young man, who had been tricked into something he didn't understand, would burst into the offices of satirical magazine Charlie Hebdo and murder its employees. En route, the young man, Cherif Kouachi, and his brother would gun down a Muslim police officer. By the time the Kouachi brothers were killed by police they had taken 12 lives.[2]

In the days that followed, another member of the Buttes-Chaumont[3] network and a childhood friend of the Kouachis',

[1] 'Paris Terror Suspect Shown in 2005 Film', *New York Times*, 8 January 2015, available at: https://www.nytimes.com/video/world/europe/100000003437718/paris-terror-suspect-shown-in-2005-film.html

[2] 'Charlie Hebdo attack: Three days of terror', *BBC News*, 14 January 2015, available at: https://www.bbc.co.uk/news/world-europe-30708237

[3] Gilles Kepel, *Terror in France: The Rise of Jihad in the West*, (Oxford, 2015), pp. 29-32. Members of Paris' Buttes-Chaumont network would go on to be involved in a number of plots, and several would travel to Iraq to fight the US-led occupation with al-Qaeda in Iraq, the precursor to ISIS.

Amedy Coulibaly, would go on to kill a police officer himself and seize hostages in a Jewish supermarket after pledging allegiance to Islamic State.[4] The professionalism and benevolence of Cherif Kouachi's social worker cannot be doubted for a moment, and no blame is to be laid at the door of this individual whatsoever. But the misplaced assumptions about the 'real reasons' for Kouachi's embrace of jihadism are indicative of a wider trend across the western world which is both harming efforts to prevent radicalisation and deradicalise offenders.

This specious trend, the belief that people are lured, manipulated, groomed or – in the words of Kouachi's benevolent social work – tricked, has not only persisted since Kouachi's attack, but actively spread among western counter-terrorism and Countering Violent Extremism (CVE) circles.

Security services may have a more realistic understanding of why and the extent to which individuals become involved in terrorism, but preventing terrorism is no longer the sole domain of security services. Non-securitised and non-coercive terrorism prevention strategies like the UK's Prevent Strategy rely on a *'whole of society approach'*,[5] one which has enlisted the support of teachers, doctors, social workers and community groups to aid in the fight against radicalisation.

This has somewhat understandably but erroneously conflated the adoption of a worldview which sanctions

---

[4] 'Paris gunman Amedy Coulibaly declared allegiance to Isis', *Guardian*, 12 January 2015, available at: https://www.theguardian.com/world/2015/jan/11/paris-gunman-amedy-coulibaly-allegiance-isis

[5] 'A Whole-of-Society Approach to Preventing and Countering Violent Extremism and Radicalization That Lead to Terrorism: A Guidebook for Central Asia', *Organization for Security and Co-operation in Europe*, 21 January 2020, available at: https://www.osce.org/secretariat/444340

mass murder – the process known as radicalisation – with phenomena such as grooming, a term usually reserved for the crime of Child Sexual Exploitation (CSE).

There has also been a widespread medicalisation of the phenomenon, with guidance and training documents produced to support the UK's Prevent Strategy to be found using terminology which might be more at home in pamphlets found in the doctor's office: with individuals, groups and communities deemed 'vulnerable' to, or 'at risk' of radicalisation.[6] There are two chief reasons for this tendency to describe radicalisation in these terms:

1. The need to secure support from public sector and community groups for counter-terrorism policies;

2. The ongoing minimisation and downplaying of Islamist ideology in explaining jihadist violence.

Framing radicalisation in the language of safeguarding and child protection has certainly helped to secure legitimacy among public sector workers who would ordinarily object to the encroachment of state counter-terrorism policy into their day jobs. It has also helped schools and institutions to easily integrate the mechanisms for making referrals alongside other safeguarding concerns. This somewhat cynical interpretation does not in any way undermine the state's legitimacy of applying non-coercive efforts to prevent radicalisation, it is merely a reflection on reality.

Sadly, this framing has gone so far that it is obscuring the reality of the threat we are all facing. The reality of why

---

[6] See, for example, the government's Educate Against Hate website, which provides information on children and young people's vulnerability to radicalisation – it is worth noting that none of the vulnerabilities listed encompass ideology: https://educateagainsthate.com/which-children-and-young-people-are-vulnerable-to-radicalisation/

thousands of westerners are not only turning their backs on liberal democracy, but actually lashing out violently against it.

On the other hand, the tendency to downplay or minimise the role of Islamist ideology as a driver in jihadist violence has also accelerated the treatment of radicalisation in this way. There are many reasons for this minimisation which are too myriad to cover in depth here: such as domestic Islamist groups downplaying the role of Islamist ideology in jihadist violence to avoid their own worldview contribution to radicalisation (even if inadvertently) coming under scrutiny. Far left groups have also played a role here, in displacing the scrutiny from ideology towards their preferred targets, such as western foreign policy.

A much larger section of liberal society though, has also sought to downplay the role of Islamist ideology in radicalisation and jihadist violence. In some cases, this has been with honourable intentions, an attempt to protect ordinary Muslims from discrimination in response to acts of terror. In other instances, it has been naivety, a secular liberal inability to conceive that people born and raised in the West could possibly hold such a worldview, and that they must really be motivated by materialistic concerns or legitimate structural grievances.[7]

This naivety was on stark display in efforts to explain the exodus of thousands of westerners to join Islamic State's millenarian project in Iraq and Syria. Commentators and analysts ascribed almost hypnotic power to Islamic State's propaganda and social media activities, once again medicalising radicalisation as though it is a condition

---

[7] Jeffrey M. Bale, 'Denying the Link between Islamist Ideology and Jihadist Terrorism: 'Political Correctness' and the Undermining of Counterterrorism', *Perspectives on Terrorism*, 2013, vol 7 (5), p. 13.

which can be caught from looking at the wrong websites – completely disregarding the network and ideological infrastructure that needed to be in place many years prior for such an exodus to be possible.[8]

Unfortunately, it seems the jihadists of Islamic State listen to us more than we listen to them. Many of the now stranded recruits who turned their back on Britain for Abu Bakr al-Baghdadi's 'Caliphate' have repeated our own delusions about being manipulated or groomed back to us via the media, which has underperformed in its duty to interrogate their claims.

To give just one example, stranded in Kurdish-run Al-Hol camp, Londoner Tooba Gondal claimed she was manipulated and never really supported Islamic State, describing herself as a 'vulnerable target for Isis recruiters'. The digital breadcrumbs left by Gondal tell a different story, with archived social media posts celebrating Jihadi John's choreographed executions and the massacre of innocent concertgoers and Friday-night revellers in Paris.[9] Far from being manipulated, Gondal herself was a recruiter, earning the tabloid nickname the 'Isis matchmaker'.[10]

Gondal's audacious claims were far from isolated among the jihadist cohorts.[11] These individuals are downplaying

---

[8] 'The Hypnotic Power of ISIS Imagery in Recruiting Western Youth', *ICSVE*, 22 April 2016, available at: https://www.icsve.org/the-hypnotic-power-of-isis-imagery-in-recruiting-western-youth-2/

[9] Simon Cottee, 'The Warped World of British Isis Fugitive Tooba Gondal', *The Spectator*, 16 October 2019, available at: https://www.spectator.co.uk/article/the-warped-world-of-the-british-isis-fugitive-tooba-gondal-

[10] Ryan Fahey, 'ISIS 'matchmaker' Tooba Gondal 'is set to be deported from Turkey to France' after she pleaded to be allowed to return to the UK', *Mail Online*, 13 November 2019, available at: https://www.dailymail.co.uk/news/article-7681093/ISIS-matchmaker-Tooba-Gondal-set-deported-Turkey.html

[11] 'Shamima Begum: IS bride says she was 'brainwashed' and wants 'a second chance'', *Sky News*, 2 April 2019, available at: https://news.sky.com/story/shamima-begum-is-bride-says-she-was-brainwashed-and-wants-a-second-chance-11681905

their own agency in their decision to join a terrorist organisation that was committing war crimes and directing massacres around the world. But this denial didn't come from nowhere – this came from us. It came from our own minimisation of agency in the 'pre-radicalisation space', which has consequently made it much more difficult to respond to those who have already passed through that very space.

The issue of the fate of stranded foreign fighters is a sensitive and emotionally charged one. While the then Home Secretary Sajid Javid opted for stripping citizenship where possible, it is unlikely that we have heard the last of these individuals. What's more many of the foreign fighters have themselves already returned to Britain (with only around 10% facing any kind of prosecution so far).[12]

Debate on the threat posed by those that have already returned, those on the run and those stranded in the hastily constructed camps and prisons of Northern Syria must be conducted with a clear eyed assessment of these individuals, and that means accepting the belief system and agency that led to their destructive decisions and the crimes they may have committed overseas.

Britain's political prisoners

The impact of the denial of agency, the minimisation of ideological belief and attempt to consider the actions of violent extremists alongside other forms of harm or crime can be seen in domestic efforts to deradicalise offenders as well.

---

[12] 'Islamic State: British Nationals Abroad:Written question – HL1240', *Parliament.uk*, 3 February 2020, available at: https://www.parliament.uk/ business/publications/written-questions-answers-statements/written-question/ Lords/2020-02-03/HL1240/

2019 London Bridge attacker Usman Khan had originally been convicted as part of a terror cell with an ambitious plot to blow up the London Stock Exchange. Released while still a young man, he joined an incredibly well-intentioned programme called 'Learning Together', run through Cambridge University, which sought to give convicted criminals opportunities and skills to help them move away from criminality.[13]

Khan, who may have been considered something of a poster-boy for this initiative, would go on to brutally murder a course coordinator and volunteer for the Learning Together programme. As criminologist Simon Cottee put it: 'He served less than half his sentence and then went on to slay those who saw the best in him.'[14]

To conduct his attack, Khan had strapped a mock suicide vest to himself. Like the London Bridge attackers of two years prior and like Sudesh Amman who would strike in Streatham weeks after Khan's rampage, the mock suicide vest gives arriving officers no choice but to use lethal force. This 'suicide by cop' tactic alone demonstrates emphatically that these are not normal criminals but individuals who see themselves as holy warriors, yearning for martyrdom and the ensuing ticket to paradise. Yes, there is often something preposterously 'Four Lions' about many of these terrorists, but it does not follow that they do not believe what they say, and what their actions imply.

Many of these terrorists are mobilising from deeply

[13] 'London Bridge attacker was poster boy for rehab scheme he targeted', *Telegraph*, 1 December 2019, available at: https://www.telegraph.co.uk/news/2019/12/01/london-bridge-attacker-poster-boy-rehab-scheme-targeted/

[14] Simon Cottee, 'Liberal Professors' Deadly Delusions About Curing Terrorists', *Foreign Policy*, 4 December 2019, available at: https://foreignpolicy.com/2019/12/04/london-bridge-attack-liberal-professors-deadly-delusions-about-curing-terrorists/

entrenched ideological milieu, rather than being radicalised alone in their bedrooms by 'slick' propaganda. Indeed, jihadist terror offenders see themselves not as criminals but as political prisoners, and they behave as such. A support network of charities and NGOs exists on the outside to lend itself to these political prisoners, and South London's extremist preacher Shakeel Begg has rallied outside HMP Belmarsh for his 'brothers'.[15]

What hopes then for deradicalisation and reintegration? We should not abandon hope, and we have no choice but to continue to try, but we must not delude ourselves about the threat these people pose, the belief systems that motivate them and the severity of the crimes they have committed.

A liberal and materialistic assumption that people who tell us they 'love death as you love life'[16] can simply be nudged back into being upstanding democratic citizens by showing them the error of their ways, offering 'opportunities and skills' or by taking part in creative writing workshops must be strictly tempered by reality.

Investing extensively in deradicalisation and 'specially trained imams', as the government has recently, is a necessary move simply because we have no other choice but to try.[17] Indeed there should be much greater focus on the theological and ideological intervention, but there is no

---

[15] 'Begg Vs BBC', *Judiciary*, 28 October 2016, available at: https://www.judiciary. uk/wp-content/uploads/2016/10/shakeel-begg-v-bbc-judgment-final-20161028. pdf

[16] *'We love death as you love life'* is a popular jihadist slogan originally attributed to an early Islamic leader. In the UK it was most famously deployed in the martyrdom video of 7/7 ringleader Mohammed Sidique Khan's martyrdom video

[17] 'Tougher sentencing and monitoring in government overhaul of terrorism response', *HM Government*, 21 January 2020, available at: https://www.gov. uk/government/news/tougher-sentencing-and-monitoring-in-government-overhaul-of-terrorism-response

'level three certificate' in deradicalisation to be attained, and men with the experience and credibility of the likes of former Afghan Mujahideen turned intervention provider Manwar Ali cannot be mass produced.[18]

Jihadists are not misled or manipulated, they are the most radically violent offshoots of a global movement called Islamism, and they have agency in their decisions. Even if it is one that most Muslims reject, the Islamist movement is an intellectually and theologically coherent movement which must be respected as an adversary by democratic states. Its adherents are often educated, articulate and compassionate individuals, driven by what they believe is morally necessary. Their vision however, is diametrically opposed to the values we hold dear in the western world.

In the coming years, Britain and Europe will see thousands of convicted extremists back on the streets to complement returnees from the Syrian jihad. Despite low recidivism rates historically, the threat is very real.[19] Our hopes of successfully reintegrating these individuals will be drastically improved if we abandon the notion that they don't know or believe what they're doing.

---

[18] Muhammad Manwar Ali was previously a prominent recruiter for the Afghan jihad against the Soviets who now dedicates his life to preventing radicalisation. Manwar Ali is also an 'intervention provider' working one on one with those at risk of radicalisation and extremist offenders

[19] Liam Duffy, 'Jihadism and Recidivism', *European Eye on Radicalization*, 15 May 2020, available at: https://eeradicalization.com/jihadism-and-recidivism/

Locked in failed ideas? Violent Islamic extremism, liberal rehabilitation and imprisonment
James Treadwell

Violent extremism is but one threat that the justice system and its agencies face. Rapidly changing organised crime now includes cyber-enabled threat such as the pernicious use of the internet to groom and abuse the young and or aid in the commission of serious offences (as capacity is enhanced by criminals exploiting encrypted communications, dark web anonymity and cryptocurrencies) which link with the challenge of Violent Extremism (VE) and the terror-related offending. The threat of all VE plays out against a context and worsens with the seeming ever growing political polarisation we witness both nationally and internationally. The overlaps between VE and organised crime have been gaining increased academic attention for several years.[1]

In England and Wales, the proportion of Muslim prisoners held in custody increased from 8% in 2002 to 16% in 2018, while for two decades a growing reactive racism formed particularly in disadvantaged white working-class communities.[2] While structural exclusion may be one feature

---

[1] Katharine Petrich, 'Cows, Charcoal, and Cocaine: Al-Shabaab's Criminal Activities in the Horn of Africa', *Studies in Conflict & Terrorism*, 17 October 2019, available at: https://doi.org/10.1080/1057610X.2019.1678873

[2] Simon Winlow, Steve Hall and James Treadwell, *The Rise of the Right: English Nationalism and the Transformation of Working-Class Politics* (Bristol, 2017)

of some radicalisation, narratives of personal victimisation and experience of racial 'others' features in an array of the biographies of all those drawn to most VE. While not all VE offenders are involved in other criminal subcultures, many are. It is worth remembering that street level and less sophisticated entry points into organised crime, like VE can be a chaotic, violent, crime linked upbringing.

In a study of young Muslim men's pathways into crime, Qasim (2017) suggests that for some involvement in drug dealing there is the ability to adapt the way they follow their faith somewhat selectively.[3] They can be anchored by their religion and family loyalty but can also make up their own rules. Hence, selling heroin is acceptable, or not considered *haram*, even if it is by elders or Imams in the mosque where they attend Friday prayers. Further, Webster and Qasim suggest in a context for example where young Islamic men have experienced an intergenerational shift in the nature and character of available employment, from skilled, stable, local high-waged, industrial (often textile based) to precarious, intermittent, low paid and low skilled service sector work, the rejection of a licit wage labour and embrace of illicit entrepreneurial criminality is hardly surprising. This is not dissimilar to what drives young, urban White and Black men toward criminality. The academic literature on VE is often explained through the presence of a melting pot of social deprivation, organised crime, and illegal drugs markets. Radical Islamic views and the pursuit of money might superficially seem counter to the ideology of much instrumental criminality, but the reality can be far from

---

[3] Mohammed Qasim, 'Explaining young British Muslim men's involvement in heroin and crack', *Criminology & Social Justice*, 2018, vol. 18 (3), pp. 349-363. Available at: https://journals.sagepub.com/doi/pdf/10.1177/1748895817704024

that, and the division between ideological and instrumental motivations are not always clear cut.[4]

Certainly we know of young men leaving the UK with Islam for Dummies in their backpack to join Daesh in Syria are as likely radicalised as much by the romanticised image of death, the glorification of violence, a heterosexual and machismo ethic, and the quest for excitement as they are any deeply held knowledge of their faith.[5] Indeed, such things are common pulls for young, misguided men who are on a path searching for meaning and find it in crime. Those factors might also explain equally well why, for example, the youthful and now outlawed Neo-Nazi group National Action (NA). Likewise, other former neo-Nazis in prison have gone on to embrace extremist Islam and become jihadis, suggesting again that there may be similarities rather than differences in the psychological profile and drivers of extremists.

Certainly, a hatred of the state, liberal democracy, along with a hatred of 'the other' is hardening in the wings of some prisons. Most extremists, and many serious criminals, demonstrate some degree of what psychologists term 'obsessive ideation', essentially a way of describing the ideas that justify violence and underlie extreme notions of othering and differentiating those they target. For instance, the notion that all westerners, or all Muslims, or all Jewish people are evil and deserving of harm. For all the growth in academic concern with prisons they have become more dangerous. There are frequent reports of drugs, weapons

---

[4] Bogdan Panayotov, 'Crime and terror of social exclusion: The case of 13 imams in Bulgaria', *European Journal of Criminology*, 2019, vol. 16 (3), pp. 369-387. Available at: https://journals.sagepub.com/doi/pdf/10.1177/1477370819829650

[5] Simon Cottee, 'The Western Jihadi Subculture and Subterranean Values, *The British Journal of Criminology*, 2020, vol. 60 (3), pp. 762-781. Available at: https://academic.oup.com/bjc/article/60/3/762/5670743

and mobile phones making their way into high security prisons. There has been scant discussion of policing and securing such spaces or seeing them as likely sites of crime. Indeed, many remain places for doing business for the most serious and dangerous of offenders.[6]

Killing rehabilitation

However, while there may be similarities between VIE (Violent Islamic Extremism), VEs (Violent Extremism) and serious criminals, there are also some very notable differences. For example, Usman Khan, who murdered Jack Merritt and Saskia Jones and seriously injured several others at the Cambridge University Institute of Criminology event at Fishmonger Hall last year before he was shot dead by police when attending an alumni celebration of the Learning Together programme. Khan would seem purely driven by extremist ideology, but we perhaps ought to spend some time considering how such offenders are identified and managed on the risk they are assessed to pose. Many thought Khan presented little threat. He was, after all invited to a profile event as a rehabilitation success story. Yet while we seemingly have serious offenders (both organised criminals and violent extremists) who pose a live significant threat, are highly capable or active in criminality, and whose actions may have a high impact on community safety and/or prison security, we might rightly ask if at present there is sufficient recognition of this in England and Wales.

Programmes such as 'Learning Together' are in keeping with the dominant liberal disposition in and around

---

6   Winlow, Hall and Treadwell, *Rise of the Right* (2017); Kate Gooch and James Treadwell, 'Prisoner Society in an Era of Psychoactive Substances, Organized Crime, New Drug Markets and Austerity', *The British Journal of Criminology*, March 2020. Available at: https://doi.org/10.1093/bjc/azaa019

criminology. To state that is hardly controversial. This liberalism tends to the topics criminologists select for study, the questions posed, the subjects taught to students, the dominant political outlook. Criminology is left-leaning politically, characterised predominantly by a distrust for prison and a determination to see it used as an institution of last resort, a scepticism towards the state and its potential abuse of power, and recognition of the importance of checking and constraining its functions and operations of the state through the rule of law and human rights. Added to this is a liberal tendency to regard penal welfarism focused on rehabilitation as suitable for all offenders, all of whom are not evil, but rather can be changed and merely need to be brought back to the good.

The issue here, is that such biases might create blind spots when it comes to some forms of criminal conduct, including violent theistic (religious) forms of extremism.[7] Does this create a discipline naively primed for exploitation and manipulation in some instances? It has been reported that Khan penned a letter from prison prior to his attack suggesting:

> 'I would like to do such a course so I can prove to the authorities, my family and society (sic) in general that I don't carry the views I had before my arrest and also I can prove that at the time I was immature, and now I am much more mature and want to live my life as a good Muslim and also a good citizen of Britain'.

Did the letter serve a greater purpose in assessing his suitability for release? Were such words alone taken as

---

[7] Simon Cottee, 'Liberal Professors' Deadly Delusions About Curing Terrorists', *Foreign Policy*, 4 December 2019, available at: https://foreignpolicy.com/2019/12/04/london-bridge-attack-liberal-professors-deadly-delusions-about-curing-terrorists/

evidence of his change? Might such sentiments as Khan's be skilfully deployed as a means of faking rehabilitation?

Indeed, it would seem likely that Khan changed little in prison but went on a rather effective journey to persuade *some* people that he had. That might however make his ultimate target more sinister. Having faked rehabilitation, it may not be insignificant that Khan targeted the group that he did; leading intellectuals and young university students from Cambridge University along with a collective of sympathetic civil servants and employees of Her Majesties Prison and Probation Service who were celebrating the virtues of a rehabilitative initiative.

What was Khan striking at when he attacked? Was it the individuals, the system, or liberal ideology? Given his own fundamental interpretation of Islam, was he striking out at and mocking the very idea of rehabilitation itself? We need to consider the belief system and views of VIEs, and criminal justice understandings and responses to them. The former often hold view the antithesis of those working in the latter. The VIEs opposes democracy, the rule of law, individual liberty and mutual respect and tolerance of different faiths and beliefs. In Iraq and Syria, Daesh justice had little time for rehabilitation or due process, comprising as it did of child executions, rape of Yazidi women, amputations, streamed beheadings, crucifixions and cage burnings; a criminal process where god mandates the death of individuals on charges of adultery, sorcery, drug dealing, blasphemy and murder as they regard proscribed in the religious text. Certainly, one speculates it is a notion of justice far removed from that debated on the Cambridge course.

That programme was formed in 2014 at HMP Grendon, a therapeutic community prison in Buckinghamshire. The Cambridge programme was set up shortly after criminologists at a rival Durham University had started to publicise to criminology that they had delivered a remarkably similar programme, but in the case of the latter, in the form of a franchise model exported from the US. That course 'Learning Together' was long tested, its focus on racial disparity in justice, but which has very different ground rules to those being used by Cambridge. There are some significant differences between the two schemes, not least that 'Inside-Out' programme offers a longer track record and more selective criteria in terms of eligible prisoners and ground rules in perusing its similar aims of social change through transformative education.

Learning Together was set up in 2014 by academics Ruth Armstrong and Amy Ludlow from the Institute of Criminology at Cambridge. Armstrong worked as a post-doctoral researcher on a project entitled *'Locating and Building Trust in a Climate of Fear: Religion, Moral Status, Prisoner Leadership and Risk in Maximum Security Prisons'*. The programme's co-founder, Ludlow is a Director of the Institute of Criminology's master's degree. Both have extensive experience with prison staff and prisoners. However, while the aims of the scheme are laudable and many have benefitted from it (including the prisoners who intervened to stop Khan) the scheme was quickly to become the targets of a highly critical article that lambasted 'Liberal Professors' Deadly Delusions About Curing Terrorists'. It made strong criticisms of the naivety and limitations of criminology when it came specifically to Islamist extremists, and observed of criminology:

> 'that it has very little to teach us about such individuals, other than a sort of negative (liberal) wisdom: Don't stigmatize; don't judge; don't label. It tells us that moral character is a bourgeois fiction or social construct, that prison is inhumane,

and that offenders should be given a second chance and helped, given the supposedly systemic obstacles that so many have faced. And it has next to nothing to say about the criminal justice response to a category of person who believes that anyone who doesn't follow the literal word of God, as set out in their favored religious texts, should be ritually slaughtered' (Cottee, 2018: np).

While Cottee's scathing criticisms of liberal naivety of criminology found favour with very few in academia, they raise some pertinent questions about the nature of contemporary criminological scholarship confronted with a serious and evolving threat of sophisticated, dangerous criminals including VIEs. It also raises the question as to whether a sensible middle ground is necessary, one that while holding onto all the aspirations of rehabilitation, focuses first and foremost on security, safety and risk management.

Rehabilitating the violent extremist?

Irrespective of the questions concerning Khan's target and intent, there is the issue of how he came to be in the middle of a conference featuring the leading intellectuals and some of the most senior figures in the prison service, armed and primed to kill at a time when the state had had near two decades worth of warnings about the potential for such a thing to happen. This is perhaps where we might consider interrogating Cottee's accusations against liberal complacency again and consider just what brought us to a point where such an attack could happen.

In the last twenty years, there has been something of a surge in the popularity of prisons research, particularly in England and Wales. This expansion has largely focused on the multifaceted harms experienced by prisoners (and their families), as well as the way the exercise of State power can often be excessive, capricious and damaging. Yet, there has also been a tendency to somewhat romanticise prisoners or to underplay the harms that they have done or may do. Confronting the latter, some criminologists have called for a more considered appraisal of why some individuals engage in serious criminality, a return to questions of motivation and a consideration of why some individuals feel they have the right to harm others in pursuit of their own goals.

We might then ask whether such considerations are apparent, for example, in Cambridge's work 'Locating trust in a climate of fear: religion, moral status, prisoner leadership, and risk in maximum security prisons' in which Alison Liebling and her Cambridge Prison Research Centre colleagues suggested of their work on the High Security estate that:

> 'A preoccupation with abstract concepts of risk in some high security prisons in particular can generate the kind of anger and alienation among prisoners that criminal justice practices should aim to avoid' (Leibling et al, 2015: 16).

While Leibling and colleagues may have a point, it is also notable that much of the academic work skirts quickly over any issues where prisoners do inflict harms. We might ask, should the most highly secure custodial places in the country, those holding potentially the most dangerous, deceptive, devious offenders not be preoccupied with risk? Is risk in such places ever merely only an abstract concept? While it is logical that most rational people would seek to avoid increasing unnecessary anger, alienation or resentment amongst a dangerous prisoner cohort, it is hardly illogical to think that more secure prisons holding long term prisoners should be concerned with at least creating the most crime free and secure environment possible? Do they do this?

It is widely acknowledged that violent extremists in prison constitute a significant ongoing threat both in custody and outside Violent Islamist Extremist prisoners tend to organise around an Emir, the prisoner who controls a self-styled Sharia court to sit in judgment on the other prisoners, sometimes presiding over ISIS pledges of allegiance and punishment beatings. One of the names to circulate in the press in this role is that of Brusthom Ziamani of HMP Woodhill, the man recently implicated in the attempted murder of a prison officer. Yet if we turn to the Cambridge research and how this role is described in the high security estate, it is almost as if it is a democratically selected position merely empowering a benign individual for social democratic ends:

> 'The necessity of the Emir was justified by recognition that the leader must be someone who was not a 'hothead', but someone who was reflective, calm and knowledgeable: 'that judge, in our situation, would be someone with the knowledge. [The judge] would be…the most respected Muslim on the wing'. 'You go the person with the highest deen [faith]' for advice. 'Character' and a peace-making ability is important alongside Islamic knowledge'. 'You pick someone who is very peaceful, a person *who doesn't like violence''*.[8]

This seems quite oblivious to the reality that it is not uncommon for covert counter-terrorism investigations to start within prisons, and that there may be some issues with extremism in prison that require a better understanding than what prisoners claim. To be fair, in many ways, the prison

---

[8] Alison Liebling, Ruth Armstrong, Richard Bramwell and Ryan Williams, 'Locating trust in a climate of fear: religion, moral status, prisoner leadership, and risk in maximum security prisons', *Prison Research Centre*, Institute of Criminology, University of Cambridge, 2015. Available at: https://www.prc. crim.cam.ac.uk/publications/trust-report

service can now claim that it is attempting to deal with the problem of VIE with faith-based approaches including Al Furqan programme where prison Imams challenge the views of VIEs through the teaching of the religion. But there is also still concern in some quarters that the Ministry of Justice has shown a reticence to recognise the pressing need to be more concerned about security and still tends to prioritise a softer rehabilitative aim.

Many prisons are hotbeds for violence, illicit markets and poor staff control. While traditionally the high security estate has fared slightly better in avoiding the disorder that have blighted local prisons, there is increasing evidence that control is slipping even there. What is likely is that unsafe and disorderly prisons aggravate the conditions that make prisoners vulnerable to reoffending and radicalisation. Extremists, like organised criminals, thrive in the vacuum that is created when prison staff withdraw or are not in control. It may be far easier for VEs to find power when the state fails to provide prisoners with basic safety or security, let alone the meaningful activities towards which their energies can be directed. Crowded and under-resourced prisons are hardly conducive to any rehabilitation, let alone those with the most fervent and entrenched ideological beliefs. Indeed, quite the opposite is true and crime in prisons has become a considerable problem.[9]

While the rehabilitation of offenders is a key feature of the system, in England and Wales, decent and legitimate prisons in which prisoners are respected by staff and where a settled and stable regime is the norm are now something

---

[9] James Treadwell, Kate Gooch and Georgina Barkham Perry, 'Crime in Prisons: Where now and where next?' (2019). Available at: http://eprints.staffs.ac.uk/5438/1/OPCC%20-%20Plan-to-government-to-tackle-organised-crime-in-prisons.pdf

or a rarity. While officials, particularly those in the Ministry of Justice can talk of rehabilitative culture in idealistic terms, many establishments are anything but.[10] Austerity, budgetary cuts, and then voluntary redundancy took away experienced frontline staff. Too few boots on the landings have made for violent, dirty prisons where conflicts over toilet rolls and clean undergarments merge with far more serious conflicts between serious criminal groups and violent extremists. Prisoners compete in the prison sub-rosa economy for market dominance, and racial tensions and religious segregation can also feature. Such a view is now filtering into some accounts of prison life but even here, there is a tendency to regard the problem and issues and modus operandi as either shaped around beliefs or around instrumental drivers.

That divide is naïve. The emergence of a hybrid group of Islamist criminal/terrorist prisoners proves that. Some participants in these are coerced by staunch terrorist offenders who have established a power base and reputation for serious violence, either personally or by delegating this role to enforcers.[11] These offenders have involved themselves in typical subversive mainstream prison behaviour such as drug and mobile phone trafficking. Recruitment can be pursued by influencing those from a criminal background to accept that Islam is a means of laundering their criminality, assuming status, gaining protection or simply pursuing their criminal activities, or individuals involvement can be

---

[10] 'Guidance: Rehabilitative culture in prisons', *HM's Prison and Probation Service*, 15 May 2019. Available at: https://www.gov.uk/guidance/rehabilitative-culture-in-prisons

[11] Monica Lloyd, 'Learning from Casework and the Literature', *Prison Service Journal*, September 2012, No. 203, pp. 23-30. Available at: https://www.crimeandjustice.org.uk/sites/crimeandjustice.org.uk/files/PSJ%20September%202012%20No.%20203.pdf

cultivated through intimidation or threat. While there can be the perception that Violent Islamic Extremism is different to serious organised crime for profit, run from or in prison, this may not always be the case. Unpicking the strands is hugely complex.

'Perhaps we can somehow turn your misguided and evil actions'

Ten days after the London bridge attack Darryn Frost, a communications manager for Her Majesty's Prison and Probation Service (HMPPS), who was at the prisoner rehabilitation event at Fishmonger Hall left a written message to Usman Khan near the site of his death. Frost had fought with Khan, stabbed him with a narwhal tusk and protected Khan from punches while he restrained him on the floor. The sentiments Frost expressed above concluded with the hope that some good, and not more hate, would be the result of Khan's crimes.[12]

There is much to commend the notion of rehabilitation. But considering the attacks, the Government introduced emergency legislation in February 2020 to end the automatic early release of terrorist offenders and made commitments to make sure no terror offender was released early without a thorough risk assessment by the Parole Board. This was met with some concern from the commentariat. The development and delivery of a co-ordinated, multi-faceted approach to assessing, managing and rehabilitating terrorist offending is still in its infancy. However, while a great deal of attention is given to the technocratic and functional process

---

[12] "You were a pawn': London Bridge hero's message to attacker', *Guardian*, 10 January 2020, available at: https://www.theguardian.com/uk-news/2020/jan/10/you-were-a-pawn-london-bridge-attack-darryn-frost-message

of how rehabilitation or deradicalisation might be done, less attention and thought has been given to the culture and climate of delivery.

The rehabilitative branch of the criminal justice system comes in the form of the National Probation Service (NPS) and its employees are largely (indeed disproportionately) white, middle class and female. There has been a tendency for modern probation workers to regard their role more as 'symbolic victim' in terms of confronting and holding offenders to account (Mawby and Worrall 2013:137). However, with what we also know about Islamist extremism, will approaches like these to rehabilitate be likely to engage, let alone prove successful? When Salman Abedi, for example, detonated his suicide bomb at the Ariana Grande concert in Manchester in May 2019, killing seventeen females (and five males), he did so secure in the knowledge it would be teenage girls and young women most likely killed. Some have argued that this deliberate targeting of women by Islamist Extremists is because in their minds they represent empowerment and enlightenment, and also immodesty, and there is clearly a misogyny, power and control ideology that regards female empowerment as an evil that must be eradicated. Yet a point worth making here is simply this, as currently constituted, much of the system geared toward rehabilitation is also a target for some ultra-conservative Islamists who want little contact with the values of forgiveness, change and positive human change, development and reconciliation.

The current threat concerning VIE does not mean we should just abandon rehabilitative aims, but perhaps we need to be much more sensible, realistic, considered and objective than merely to think that change in such harmful individuals as Khan should be taken on face value. We may need to have more considered discussions about how they might be challenged, and who should do that challenging, how long it may take and how it may need a degree of deprivation of liberty and safeguard against abuse.

A core feature of Western Jihadi Subculture (and associated VIE) is wholly at odds with the violent far-right for example, in what is termed disdain for the Dunya. The 'dunya' is the current material, temporal world: the world of earthly concerns and possessions in the here-and-now, as opposed to the world of the hereafter – that is, the eternal world of punishment or paradise that awaits us after we die. For VIEs, the dunya is essentially worthless. Hence the institution of the prisons may have a very valid roles, it protects most of the public from dangerous people such as Khan. Some VIEs clearly possesses a mental infrastructure that allows the intent to do horrific violent deed whether in prison or in the community. All this then begs the question; for some of the most dangerous violent extremists, is long term incapacitation as a form of public protection simply just a better immediate end? Should we be willing to lock some extremists up near permanently?

Clearly some VIEs, like Khan, will prove impervious to deradicalisation or rehabilitation, but they may fake compliance with it well. In such instances, there may always be some risk and danger built into the system, and it may prove important to have a sensible debate that acknowledges that some degree of fallibility in the justice process always has existed, and likely ever will. That does not mean we should abandon a rehabilitative aspiration, just as Darryn Frost noted. Better questions than the standard, 'how do we rehabilitate violent extremists?' for me include can we feel confident that Jihadi argot with its uses and euphemisms, such as 'cake-baking' [making explosives] or 'Green birds' [martyrs], is known widely by prison and probation staff who work with the men who use them? Are we probing enough about their intent and their views? Do we need a mechanism in some instances to increase detention for public protection?

Many extremists do have their ideology and beliefs well mastered, but they also know their opponents well. It would seem the same is not true in reverse. Violent extremists often understand the thinking of their western liberal enemies. As suggested here, it may help them to weaponise and exploit that weakness against them. Yet we must not simply allow the risks of feigned compliance to push us fully away from a goal of rehabilitation and human change, even if that goal is one that we continually work to reaffirm and regard as feint. In the end, we perhaps still need to work for rehabilitation, but be much more pragmatic and realistic about achieving that goal. Perhaps like the tone of Frost's letter, we need a doubtful, sceptical and realistic view. Because rehabilitation represents something VIEs wish to kill, we must reaffirm faith in it. It must be a faith built on both more knowledge, and a greater degree of scepticism.

CIVITAS

Our Aims and Programmes

- We facilitate informed public debate by providing accurate factual information on the social issues of the day, publishing informed comment and analysis, and bringing together leading protagonists in open discussion. Civitas never takes a corporate view on any of the issues tackled during the course of this work. Our current focus is on issues such as education, health, crime, social security, manufacturing, the abuse of human rights law, and the European Union.

- We ensure that there is strong evidence for all our conclusions and present the evidence in a balanced and objective way. Our publications are usually refereed by independent commentators, who may be academics or experts in their field.

- We strive to benefit public debate through independent research, reasoned argument, lucid explanation and open discussion. We stand apart from party politics and transitory intellectual fashions.

- Uniquely among think tanks, we play an active, practical part in rebuilding civil society by running schools on Saturdays and after-school hours so that children who are falling behind at school can achieve their full potential.

Subscriptions and Membership

For subscriptions and membership forms, go to:
https://www.civitas.org.uk/subscriptions-and-membership/
or call (0)20 7799 6677

Book Subscriptions – £35 a year (UK only): If you would like to
stay abreast of Civitas' latest work, you can have all of our books
delivered to your door as soon as they are published.

Friends of Civitas – £25 special offer for the first year (UK only):
As a Friend of Civitas you will receive all of our publications –
including not only our books but all online releases – throughout
the year.

Renewals for Existing Members: If you are an existing member
who has previously paid via cheque or using our internal form
but would like to renew with the ease and convenience of PayPal,
please access the link above.

Make a Donation: If you like our work and would like to help
see it continue, please consider making a donation.

Supporters of Civitas: If you would like to support our work on
a rolling basis, there is a variety of advanced membership levels
on offer.

Forms can be either faxed to
+44 (0)20 7799 6688 or posted to:

Civitas: Institute For The Study Of Civil Society
First Floor
55 Tufton Street
Westminster
London
SW1P 3QL.

Please make cheques payable to Civitas.
Email: subs@civitas.org.uk

Civitas is a registered charity, No. 1085494